"Katie has written a must-reac
church communication world.
needed to succeed in our rapidly changing world of communication—
everything from social media, creating a persona, and incorporating
the paid, earned, shared, and owned (PESO) model. This is your
opportunity to learn from one of the best!"

—*Jen Bennett,* assistant professor of strategic communication at
Indiana Wesleyan University

"When Katie and I served on the staff of Brentwood Baptist Church,
I would walk down the hall and ask her questions about social media,
emerging technology, and how the church should respond to these
emerging challenges and opportunities. Katie may no longer serve
with me at Brentwood Baptist Church, but she's not on your church
staff either. So, do what I'm doing: buy this book. It's the next best
thing to walking down the hall to Katie's office."

—*Mike Glenn,* senior pastor at Brentwood Baptist Church

"This is *the* church communication book I needed. As a senior
pastor, I am asking all my key leaders to read it, and then we will
use it as a master guide to develop strategies for all our social media,
communications, and digital presence. Katie has given us the essential
tools to know how to communicate in the new realities of our world.
Strongly recommended."

—*Bobby Harrington,* pastor and chief executive officer of
Discipleship.org and Renew.org

"This is a great textbook for anyone interested in working in church
communications or marketing in general. This is a research-driven
textbook combining foundational marketing concepts that have been
customized for the church. She covers SMART goals, SWOT analysis,
segmentation, market research for targeting mailings, big data, and
branding. She goes into details about Google Local SEO, content
strategy, email marketing, and so much more. I review marketing
resumes on a regular basis. If I know a candidate has been through this
book, they would have a great advantage in my mind."

— *Jamie Stahler,* vice president of marketing, sales, and
partnerships at Outreach, Inc.

"Finally! A book that focuses more on strategy than tactics. Effective church communications start with an effective strategy. Whether you're a marketing veteran or just getting started, buckle up as Katie teaches you how to build a customized church communications strategy."
—*Holly Tate,* senior vice president of growth at Leadr

"Katie has written a must-read primer for anyone wanting to understand what church communications looks like in a rapidly evolving digital era."
—*Justin Trapp,* founder of Ministry Pass

"Katie has created another invaluable resource for church communicators, especially those new to strategic communication management. Informed by her own experience as a marketing professional and educator, this book simplifies the multifaceted responsibilities for those who are doing this important work in the church. Each chapter has real examples and practical tips that make the book easy to read, understand, and use. New or seasoned church communicators will want to read and keep this resource at hand for easy reference as they serve their church."
—*Kevin S. Trowbridge,* department chair of public relations at Belmont University

CHURCH
COMMUNICATIONS

CHURCH COMMUNICATIONS

METHODS AND MARKETING

Katie Allred

ACADEMIC
NASHVILLE, TENNESSEE

ISBN: 978-1-0877-3017-2

Dewey Decimal Classification: 254.3
Subject Heading: MASS MEDIA / TELECOMMUNICATION / SOCIAL
NETWORKING

Cover design by Darren Welch.

Printed in the United States of America
27 26 25 24 23 22 VP 1 2 3 4 5 6 7 8 9 10

Dedication

To . . .

my mom, who took me to church and cooked for and
fed those who came every Sunday, without whom
ChurchCommunications.com would not be a reality today;

my late father, who told me that getting a
business degree would help the church;

my brother and his wife, my biggest fans
and constant sources of friendship;

my friends who always said I would write a
book one day and never doubted;

my business partner, Kenny Jahng, who never gave up on
our dream of serving thousands of churches worldwide;

and to you, Church Communicator, for giving me a chance.

Contents

Acknowledgments

Without some of my friends and colleagues from around the world, this book would not have been written. I would like to thank the following people for their contributions to this book and valuable feedback to shape this first edition.

- Kenny Jahng, Big Click Syndicate, and Church Communications
- Lydia McMillan, Church Communications
- Natalie Evers
- Derek Hanson, Christ Community Church
- Tessa Morrell, LifeWay Christian Resources
- Darrel Girardier, Brentwood Baptist Church
- Mike Glenn, Brentwood Baptist Church
- Abby McCully, Church Communications
- Kaitlin Danhour, Church Communications
- Hannah Didier, Church Communications
- Avery Wilhite, Church Communications
- Hannah Teryn, Church Communications
- Nona Jones, Nona Jones Ministry
- Jim Baker, Sacred Structures
- Kadi Cole, Kadi Cole & Company

- Scott Magdalein, ServeHQ
- Jeanette Yates, Text In Church
- Brady Shearer, ProChurchTools
- Ellen Graeber Knight, Faith Fellowship Church
- Sandy Hughes, Central Peninsula Church
- Todd Greer, University of Mobile
- Kathy Dunning, University of Mobile
- The many members of the Church Communications Facebook Group

Thank you.

Introduction

When I think about why church communication is needed today, I think about the more than 30,000 church leaders in our ever-growing Facebook Group, Church Communications. When I started ChurchCommunications.com in 2015, I thought I would find fifty people who would want to commiserate over creating the church bulletin each week. What I found was much deeper than that.

Churches across the world are now engaged in our community. Our group is highly engaged—around 80 percent of those 30,000 people in our group use it every single day. We were wrong, and I am more than happy to admit that.

We are moving toward an exciting time when we can communicate with our church members and people far from Christ in just a moment from anywhere in the world, as long as we have an Internet connection. We have never been more connected, but we've also never been lonelier. A 2019 study of more than 10,000 American adults by Cigna found that "three in five Americans [61 percent] reported sometimes or always feeling alone" and "half of Americans rarely or never [feel] as though there are people who understand them."[1]

A recent article from *Psychology Today* stated, "Generation Z (those born after about 1995) was found to be the loneliest generation. And social media use alone is not a predictor of loneliness. In all the findings, a lack of meaningful human connectedness is paramount."[2] The lack of human connection is staggering, and it seems the COVID-19 pandemic has only made it worse.

It was the end of 2019 when I was asked to write this book, and I received the contract in the first couple of months of 2020, right before the pandemic started. When the pandemic forced churches worldwide to close their physical doors, I watched many congregations struggle to figure out how to reach people when they could not do it in person. This book does not focus on the subject of the online church per se, but I have included many online strategies.

Why does the online church matter to me? When I was nine years old, I started a Harry Potter forum with some friends from all over the world; this weird corner of the Internet gained international fame. Through it, I learned to create real, meaningful relationships online that genuinely mattered and made a difference. As a child, I shared the gospel intentionally and clearly with thousands of people online. I typically say that I did it "on purpose and by accident."

So how can we as a global church reach lonely people? How can we take the gospel forward in new and exciting ways? I think the answer is in new and better communication. Our churches should not have to guess what we are going to talk about next; let's plan it strategically so the gospel can reach the ends of the earth.

---

[1] "Loneliness and the Impact," Cigna, accessed September 21, 2021, https://www.cigna.com/static/www-cigna-com/docs/health-care-providers/resources/loneliness-index-provider-flyer.pdf.

[2] Frank J. Ninivaggi, "Loneliness: A New Epidemic in the USA," *Psychology Today,* February 12, 2019, https://www.psychologytoday.com/us/blog/envy/201902/loneliness-new-epidemic-in-the-usa.

Chapter 1

Marketing Strategy

We all have to deal with marketing in our daily lives. You may have driven a car that you saw advertised online. You may have gone to a big box store because they were having a sale. You may have eaten at a restaurant and were surprised at how expensive your final bill was. Why? Marketing is the reason.

Seth Godin, author of *This Is Marketing,* says, "Marketing used to be a side effect. We had a factory, [and] it was busy. We said to the marketing team, 'Here's some money; go sell average stuff to average people.' [That is] not true anymore. Marketing is at the core of what we do. . . . Marketing is the story you tell."[1]

Marketing affects all aspects of a company's operations. Many great companies have grown or failed due to their marketing plans, or lack thereof. You may have experienced the power of great marketing more than a few times. This is why marketing is more than just a social media campaign—it is a marketing strategy. All marketing involves an exchange of value. Many things are valuable. We immediately think of money, but time and data also have value.

[1] Seth Godin, "What Is Marketing Today? With Seth Godin," YouTube, December 19, 2019, video, 4:39, https://www.youtube.com/watch?v=vrJY85dBJLc.

Marketing is defined by the American Marketing Association as "the activity, set of institutions, and processes for creating, communicating, delivering, and exchanging offerings that have value for customers, clients, partners, and society at large."[2]

Good marketing requires planning and action, so a marketing strategy plan must be in place to define the marketing activities for a specific period. Furthermore, such a project must be segmented. In *Building a StoryBrand*, Donald Miller makes a great point: "Customers don't generally care about your story; they care about their own."[3] People care about their stories. To phrase it in more spiritual terms, people care about the story that God is crafting within them. They want to have a significant role in God's story. They want to tell a great story about their lives.

The problem is that many times it's the church that wants to be the great story. The church often sees itself as the hero of the story, but we as marketers and church leaders need to make the story about the person we are trying to reach and how we as a church can help that person on their journey toward being more like Christ.

The Marketing Strategy Plan

Do it right, do it light; do it wrong, do it long.
—Rex Littleton, Katie's high school history teacher

It is Monday night, and Sunday will be rolling around again before long. What does your church have planned for its marketing strategy? Does your church even have a marketing strategy? Many churches do not have a written marketing plan or marketing strategy. Even major companies are missing a marketing plan. Most churches and companies are just winging it. So, the question is: Why do they not have a marketing strategy? Most churches do not have written marketing strategies because they do not have the time or expertise. Still, every church should develop one in order to reach their community and clearly communicate the gospel of Jesus.

---

[2] "Definition of Marketing," American Marketing Association, 2017, https://www.ama.org/the-definition-of-marketing-what-is-marketing.

[3] Donald Miller, *Building a StoryBrand: Clarify Your Message so Customers Will Listen* (New York: HarperCollins Leadership, 2017), ix.

Why should you have a plan? Because planning is biblical. God planned too: "Have you not heard? I designed it long ago; I planned it in days gone by. I have now brought it to pass" (Isa 37:26). Jesus taught how we should plan using stories. Remember the wise and foolish builder:

> Therefore, everyone who hears these words of mine and acts on them will be like a wise man who built his house on the rock. The rain fell, the rivers rose, and the winds blew and pounded that house. Yet it didn't collapse, because its foundation was on the rock. But everyone who hears these words of mine and doesn't act on them will be like a foolish man who built his house on the sand. The rain fell, the rivers rose, the winds blew and pounded that house, and it collapsed. It collapsed with a great crash. (Matt 7:24–27)

The book ReTHINK.Ministry concluded that strategic planning can be advantageous to a church for many reasons.[4] First, it saves time and money. Second, it helps the church clarify its goals, vision, and mission so everyone knows what it is trying to accomplish. We know what is scheduled is what gets done. Third, strategic planning allows the church to maintain coordinated and consistent efforts. Strategic marketing planning helps the leadership team of a church know more precisely what to prioritize throughout the year.

It is essential for church staff, especially communication teams, to be proactive rather than reactive. If a church operates reactively, it is often rushed into making decisions. However, if a church has an aggressive strategic planning approach in place, it means the church leadership has a direction and knows what to say yes and no to, which gives the church ample time to make much more effective decisions. Effective strategic planning can make a massive difference in the life of a church.

Traditional Marketing vs. Church Marketing

The Four Ps, also known as the "Marketing Mix," were defined by Dhruv Grewal and Michael Levy to guide all the marketing and

---

[4] Binkley, Kathryn, "Step 0 - Strategy" in *ReTHINK.Ministry*, 2–3. RethinkMinistry.org, 2016.

communication decisions we make in traditional marketing. The Four Ps are:

1. Product
2. Price
3. Place
4. Promotion[5]

A church can use the Four Ps like this: The product could be an event. There is a price to attend the event, or maybe the event is free. There is a place for the event, and we decide that for the four weeks leading up to the event, we will promote the event via social media, email marketing, and on our website. We will also do a press release two weeks before the event.

In recent years, marketers have added three more Ps to the marketing mix: people, processes, and physical evidence.[6]

1. People create value and also *have* inherent value.
2. Processes develop value.
3. Physical evidence helps people see value.

There is another framework to add for church marketing. The Five Ws (sometimes referred to as "Five Ws and How," "5W1H," or "Six Ws") are considered necessary information-gathering questions or problem-solving questions. According to Workfront, "[The Five Ws] constitute a formula for getting the complete story on a subject. According to the principle of the Five Ws, a report can only be considered complete if it answers these questions starting with an interrogative word."[7]

Each of the five Ws (and one H) are composed of simple questions:

1. Why?
2. Who?
3. What?
4. Where?

---

[5] Dhruv Grewal and Michael Levy, *Marketing* (New York: McGraw Hill Education, 2020).

[6] Kayla Carmichael, "Extending Marketing Mix: What It Is and Why It's Useful," Hubspot, updated July 30, 2021, https://blog.hubspot.com/marketing/extended-marketing-mix.

[7] "The 5 Ws (and 1 H) That Should Be Asked of Every Project!," Workfront, May 7, 2018, https://www.workfront.com/blog/project-management-101-the-5-ws-and-1-h-that-should-be-asked-of-every-project.

5. When?
6. How?

The Five Ws and the Seven Ps are not mutually exclusive. Let's first look at the Seven Ps as they relate to an example of summer camp:

Product: Summer camp

Price: How much will summer camp cost to run? How much will it cost for students? How much will it cost for the church? What does our budget look like for camp?

Place: Where are we going to camp? (Marketing for camp will depend on where we are going. A church probably should not use a tropical theme when they are headed to the mountains.)

Promotion: How will we get students to sign up for camp? How long should we promote it? Where should we encourage it? Why should we encourage it?

People: How many campers can we serve? Who is the guest speaker? Who will lead us in worship? What will adult leaders do on this trip?

Process: What kind of experience do we want our students to have? What needs to be done before we leave? What needs to happen during camp? What needs to happen after camp?

Physical evidence: Do we have students from last year who can testify about how Jesus worked in their lives through the student camp? How did students respond this year? What can we do better next year to improve by evaluating this evidence?

This example can also fall into the 5W1H framework. We go to summer camp so that students can have a personal experience with Jesus—the *why*. Summer camp is the *what*. Student ministry is the *who*. Summer camp is held at a retreat center—the *where*. Finally, summer camp is July 9 through 14; that is the *when*. The camp program or camp facility might be the *how*.

If we use the camp example again, let us further analyze the 5W1H model with the following questions:

1. Why are we doing summer camp?
2. Who is coming to summer camp? Who will be in charge?
3. What is summer camp?
4. Where will the camp be held?
5. When is summer camp going to be held?

6. How are we doing summer camp this year? Are we traveling?
Are we going to fundraise?

These are small nuances, but the church will often need them
both. When church leaders plan an overarching 30,000-foot view of
an event, they should use the Seven Ps, but when church leaders need
detail, they should use the 5W1H. Ultimately, church leaders need
them both.

It is essential to further expand on the why. *Start with Why* by
Simon Sinek introduces the Golden Circle Theory, which explains
why some organizations make it as a company and inspire people,
while others do not.[8] The Golden Circle has three layers: the what,
the how, and the why. The outside layer is *what* an organization does;
the middle layer is *how* it does what it does; and the inner layer is
why an organization does what it does. Most people know what they
do, but very few know why they do it. Most organizations think from
the outside in, but most successful organizations think from the inside
out. Apple and Nike are examples of companies that start with why.
Apple doesn't just sell great computers and other electronics; they sell
a lifestyle. It's the same with Nike. They don't just sell shoes; they
sell athleticism. For consumers to be invested in what an organization
does, the main focus needs to be on why it does what it does.

How can we apply this to church? Churches often get bogged
down in the details and miss their why, but remember salvation is
at stake for many in their communities. You do not want to miss an
opportunity to share the gospel because you had your head down planning another event. Never forget why church leaders do what they
do—to spread the gospel.

We will dig into this as we continue through the book. It starts
with building a marketing strategy. It is personified through the
church's brand and brand messaging. Romans 8:28 says, "We know
that all things work together for the good of those who love God, who
are called according to his purpose." The *why* affects everything the
church does—including the marketing strategy, digital marketing, and
even how the church does project management. Through this work,
with God's help, we can bring it all together.

---

[8] Simon Sinek, *Start with Why: How Great Leaders Inspire Everyone to Take Action*
(London: Penguin Business, 2019).

What Is a Marketing Strategy?

A marketing strategy helps us reach people and reach our objectives. Simply put, strategic planning in marketing is the act of being intentional and clear with our goals. A church's marketing plan is a guide for preparing, implementing, and measuring its marketing strategy over a defined period of time. Despite the fact that the marketing plans for the different ministries within the church may vary, they all strive to reach the same church goals.

An excellent strategic plan will drive a congregation to focus on the unique resources and gifts God gave them in order to take full advantage of their opportunities. Scripture says, "Pay careful attention, then, to how you walk—not as unwise people but as wise—making the most of the time, because the days are evil" (Eph 5:15–16). The communication director or minister plans the marketing strategy but lets God direct the marketing.

A marketing strategy can also be referred to as a communication strategy, an outreach plan, or the church's vision plan. A marketing strategy is a guide; nobody can predict the future. The marketing strategy should be a dynamic document that evolves as time goes by.

How to Develop a Marketing Strategy for the Church

All marketing plans follow a similar framework.[9] The marketing strategy plan overview outlined in the following list is inspired by a textbook methodology found in *Marketing* by Dhruv Grewal and Michael Levy, adapted for use in the church.

- Step 1: Define the church's vision, mission, and goals.
- Step 2: Identify the strengths, weaknesses, opportunities, and threats (SWOT) of the church.
- Step 3: Understand and assess opportunities for growth via segmentation, targeting, and positioning by defining the church's verticals.

---

[9] The majority of the suggestions and strategies here are focused on technology and social media strategies. For information involving traditional methods and printed communication methods, see appendix G.

- Step 4: Apply the marketing mix through the Seven Ps or the 5W1H.
- Step 5: Evaluate performance using marketing analytics.[10]

Step 1: Define the Church's Mission, Vision, Values, and Goals

A church moves forward by being committed to its mission, vision, and values. In order of importance for a church is creating a mission statement, then a vision statement, then using those to guide the values of the church. The most crucial goal in this process is to make sure all of these parts are working together seamlessly to provide a clear picture of where the church is going next. A church is only as strong and vibrant as its people; everyone must be confident about your mission—knowing why you are doing this thing called "church." A vision gives a clear idea of where the future will take place, and the values guide how you will get there. So the mission is the "*why* we do what we do," the vision is the "where we are going," the values are the "*what* we hold dear, celebrate, and champion," and the goals are the "*how* we will do it and how we know we are making progress." Each part is fundamental for the church to move forward.

DEFINE THE CHURCH'S MISSION

A mission statement has three components: the target audience (whom you are trying to reach), the church's contribution (what ministries, missions, and services the church provides), and the church's distinctiveness (the special gifts this church has to offer the community). A mission statement should answer three questions:

1. Why do we exist?
2. What is God's purpose for our church?
3. How can we make a difference?

Following are a few practical suggestions on how to create a mission statement:

- Start with the word *to.*
- Keep it short and straightforward.

---

[10] Grewal and Levy, *Marketing,* 34.

- Think long-term.
- Ask staff for their input.
- Do not be afraid to change the mission statement as the church grows.

DEFINE THE CHURCH'S VISION

Like a mission statement, a vision statement clearly outlines the church's purpose and mission. It is a useful tool for members of the church staff and the people. A vision statement describes the long-term goals of a church, whereas a mission statement describes the who, what, and why of the church.

A congregation might ask, "What's next for our church?" In this volatile, unpredictable, but also innovative historical era, trying to predict a church's future can seem like a daunting task. Look ahead and use God's Word to plan your move forward.

The process for creating a vision statement and a mission statement is very similar. Still, it is essential that the mission statement and vision statement are written separately and distinctively so each one gets the time and recognition it deserves. Once the mission is known, a church might discover it wants to change its vision. However, first figure out what the church's vision is.

Before the church begins these processes, they might find it worthwhile to seek professional guidance to better understand what they need to do. Perhaps there is a business professional in the church who has helped create a vision statement before. If so, it might be helpful to ask them if they are able to contribute. There are also plenty of church leadership consultants like Auxano, Church Answers, or my company, Church Communications, who have helped churches across the country create a strategy for growth using this creative planning process.

DEFINE THE CHURCH'S VALUES

Values lead the activities, conduct, and objectives of the church, and they never change. Values are often deeply held convictions, principles, or priorities that influence the church's behavior or attitude. Core values are the foundation for the church's strategy. The mission and vision statements should explain the church's core values. Consider the following questions before composing the church's value statement:

1. Why do we believe what we believe?
2. Why do we act the way we do?

3. As a church, what are we dedicated to doing?

Here's an example of a mission statement, vision statement, and core values from Bellevue in Memphis, Tennessee:[11]

- *Vision statement:* We believe God is calling us to be a catalyst for spiritual awakening in Memphis and beyond.
- *Mission statement:* Our mission is to love God, love people, share Jesus, and make disciples.
- Value statements

  - *Intimacy with Jesus:* Pursuing a passionate relationship with Jesus above all
  - *Biblical Truth:* Treasuring God's perfect Word as our standard for life and faith
  - *Intentional Hospitality:* Welcoming every person with the love of Jesus
  - *Ministry Excellence:* Reflecting the character of God in service to others
  - *City Renewal:* Investing in the redemption of the people of our community

DEFINE THE CHURCH'S OBJECTIVES AND GOALS

Strategic objectives are continuous, long-term aspects of a church's mission that help the church reach its goals. The goal is to accomplish a church's mission (where the church is now) and vision (where the church is going) over a long period of time.

Objectives help set the stage, while goals bring things into focus. The vision is to be realized by achieving goals. Objectives help turn the church's mission into actions that will fulfill the church's dreams, both programmatically and organizationally. All churches should have goals. Each department should have goals that complement the church's goals, and each staff member should have plans that help accomplish their department's goals. Defining the church's goals and objectives can sound confusing, but it does not have to be—think of it as a church "goal funnel." Ministry is not, nor will it ever be, this clear-cut. For that reason, goal setting in the church needs to leave room for flexibility and patience.

---

[11] "Vision," Bellevue, August 25, 2021, https://www.bellevue.org/vision.

- At the top of the funnel are the church's overarching goals. Here is an example of an overall church goal: by 2026, we aim to baptize 100 people in lower Alabama.
- In the middle of the funnel are departmental goals. Here is an example of a departmental goal for communication: by the first quarter of next year, we will devise a digital marketing strategy and allocate a budget to reach at least 200 new people in our community.
- Then at the bottom of the funnel are individual goals. Here is an example of an individual supporting the department goals: by the second quarter of 2025, Joe Black will create and implement a Facebook advertising strategy to increase church visits by at least two new visitors per Sunday morning (2 visitors x 52 Sundays in a year = 104 people).

As each goal becomes more focused, it becomes more individualized, from the entire church to the department to the individual who will accomplish these goals. These individual staff goals are just as important as the church's overarching goals because they support the way we get there. Creating a goal funnel will help any church succeed.

Setting SMART Goals

SMART goals help organizations stay grounded and set them up for success. To help time and resource departments in churches and other ministries serve more effectively, SMART goals should be identified in each department and church. All the goals described previously in this book—church, department, and individual goals—are examples of SMART goals.[12] The acronym SMART stands for the following:

- Specific

  - "What specific goal has God set before this church?"
  - Goals are well defined and clear.
  - Ask the Five Ws: Who? What? Where? When? Why?

- Measurable

  - "How can we measure that goal?"

---

[12] Duncan Haughey, "A Brief History of SMART Goals," Project Smart, 2014, https://www.projectsmart.co.uk/brief-history-of-smart-goals.php.

- Specific standards empower the church to evaluate success in the accomplishment of its objectives.
- It is often difficult to measure things like spiritual growth, but consider measuring the church congregation's input rather than its outcomes.

- Achievable

  - "Are the church's goals achievable?"
  - Goals should be attainable and not impossible to achieve.

- Realistic/Relevant

  - Goals should be within reach and relevant to the church's purpose.
  - Whose goal is this?

    - Why is this goal important?
    - Is it Christ-centered?

- Timely/Time-Bound

  - "Does the church want to achieve this goal within a week, a month, a year?"
  - Establish goals and milestones to keep the church on track. The church should have a clearly defined start date and a clearly defined target date (deadline).
  - Time constraints create urgency.

If vision is the big picture of where one is going, goals are the operating focus areas for a set time period. Churches should create SMART goals to help fulfill the vision of the church; indeed, a church's mission or vision cannot be fulfilled without goals. The church must strive to steward the congregation's resources and time. SMART goals help organizations create goals that are clearly defined and feasible.

Step 2: Determine the Strengths, Weaknesses, Opportunities, and Threats (SWOT) of the Church

The situation analysis should be used to understand how your church is doing now and what needs improving. The SWOT acronym helps you think about internal strengths (assets) and external challenges that affect the success or failure of marketing efforts for outreach initiatives like events planning, media relations activities, etc. The potential positive impact on all these areas makes it essential to analyze where things stand currently and consider long-term possibilities by looking at opportunities available through branding strategies that can create new avenues into growth.

To begin a SWOT analysis, be sure to get the right people in the room and have plenty of room to write. The right people are any stakeholders in the church's ministry and mission. Stakeholders could include the communication team, the pastor, elders or deacons, and congregants. Try to include as much diversity as possible, meaning different ethnic groups represented in the church, as well as different genders. The environment in which the church leadership team plans is also essential and almost as important as the planning itself. Be sure to remove all distractions so the team can focus on the task at hand.

First, define the church's strengths. Strengths are internal, meaning strength comes from within the church body itself. Strengths and weaknesses are often seen as things the church may have some control over. Some examples of strength could be the church's brand, the church's resources and giving, or the church's location. Does the church have diversity? That is a strength, but if the church does not, it would be considered a weakness. Does the church offer programs, events, and ministries that reach the target market and serve the local community? What is unique about this specific church as compared to other churches in the area? What makes this specific church different from other churches around the area? Strengths in a SWOT analysis encompass what the church is fundamentally good at doing.

Weaknesses are also internal. Where is this specific church failing or not as strong? All the strengths listed in the previous paragraph could be considered weaknesses as well. Is the church's brand disjointed? Does the church have a social media presence? Does the church have a clear and compelling website? Does the church have the resources it needs to reach the local community? Is the church distinctive enough to stand out among other churches? Are the ministries and other opportunities discipling the church's congregation? Weaknesses are places where the church can do better.

Opportunities and threats are things over which the church has no control. Opportunities and threats are external or exist outside the church but still affect the church. They are areas the church has yet to venture into but could benefit from. Consider the local community and the country in which a church is located. Consider again what is going on technologically in the world. Are there advancements in technology the church needs to consider as they reach their target market? Other opportunities might exist socially, like maybe there is a new local gym growing in members that the church could partner with for a ministry opportunity. Good church leaders ask if there are some unfilled needs in the local community that the church could fill. For example, my home church in Clanton, Alabama, created a basketball gym in the early 2000s because at that time there were not a lot of things for young people to do in our area. We used that gym a lot when it was first created, and now they use it for worship, along with many other activities.

The church should consider physical opportunities as well. Perhaps there are new and growing groups of people the church can serve. For example, Brentwood, Tennessee, had a growing group of Chinese immigrants when I attended church there, and we established a Chinese congregation and hired a Chinese pastor to serve them. Another example is the deaf ministry at Brentwood Baptist Church. The church found research that there was a growing number of deaf people who were unreached in the middle-Tennessee area, so Brentwood, through Christ's prompting, began a ministry that has led to a thriving deaf church today.

Is there an opportunity to rebrand or further the church's brand awareness through various partnerships? Maybe the church can partner with local ministries and nonprofits to share resources and get the word out about the church. For example, food delivery boxes from a food pantry could include a card noting that the church donated the box. Another example is letting area schools use the church's facilities. Community service is often seen as a great partnership that increases brand awareness for many churches. Partnering with other churches might also be an opportunity if the community has a need that could be better met by pooling together resources like money and people.

Other opportunities might be found by researching if the market demand is increasing for spiritual guidance or care in the local area. Using web tools like Google Trends can help church leaders stay informed about those opportunities as they arise and create resources to meet those needs. Other questions to ask that help identify opportunities and threats might include: Will the government or current political climate affect the church positively or negatively? Are there government regulations that can be seen as an opportunity or a threat? Are there issues in the world that could affect the church?

Threats are also external issues that affect the church. They might not be as large as the government regulating the church, but they could be something like the church down the road pursuing this church's current members or people in the same target market. Could the loss of people in the church's age bracket in the community be considered a threat? For example, is a church primarily made up of older people and the area is now mostly made up of young families? The dwindling population of the target market could be seen as a threat, or it could be seen as an opportunity to reach the new young families in the local area. Consider the strengths of the top local church "competitors." In what ways are those churches better at reaching or serving the local community? Can your church create an opportunity to do something similar? Think about the strategies other churches use when reaching people in the local community. Could those strategies be considered a threat? How are people in the congregation likely to respond if and when the church markets differently based on these growing threats and opportunities? Those attitudes might be considered a threat. Do people in the local community dislike certain things about this church? That can be seen as a threat. Is the local area growing or not growing? That can also be considered a threat. Issues of bad ethical practices such as allegations of abuse in local area churches could be considered another threat.

A SWOT analysis will give church leaders a high-level view of where the church is and where the church is going. Using internal strengths and weaknesses, the church can see things it can take advantage of as well as issues the church needs to improve. Using the external opportunities and threats, the church can now make decisions that are proactive instead of reactionary.

*Step 3: Understand and Assess Opportunities for Growth
via Segmentation, Targeting, and Positioning by Defining
the Church's Verticals*

Segmentation, targeting, and positioning (STP) is a process by which
marketers clearly define the target audience they are seeking. Why
should we segment our church lists? Because each person's needs are
different. Why should we target potential guests specifically? We were
given one job as communicators of the gospel, and that is to share the
gospel in "Judea, Samaria, and the rest of the world," so we reach our
Judea by using STP. It does take more effort to do this part of the plan,
but I have often heard it said, "If you are a business for everyone, you
are a business for no one." The same can be said about the church:
while the gospel is for everyone, a church is likely to reach specific
kinds of people. Through the process of STP, we not only set our marketing goals, but we can also reach them.

SEGMENTATION

Church catering to different types of people is no easy task. But by
segmenting the church with various needs, you can keep your customers happy and satisfied! Imagine a car rental agency for an example—they have cars that are perfect for each type or consumer: The
first segment might be the "need for speed" consumer. This person is
looking for a fast car and something to show off. The second segment
might be the business casual user, which is the car rental agency's
largest segment and to whom they mostly cater. The business casual
user is looking for a decent-looking vehicle with good gas mileage.
The third tier, and often their smallest, is the "green energy" user. This
user refuses to drive anything that is a gas guzzler and only wants a
hybrid or electric car.

Considering different church ministries as different segments, or
different verticals, helps us figure out to whom we should minister
and where the growth is happening. The most common segmentation
method involves demographic information such as age, gender, family size, income, occupation, lifestyle, education level, and religion.
Many church ministries are already naturally broken down into marketing segments such as preschool, children, students, and so on. Demographic segmentation is the easiest and most common form of segmenting because it is easy to recognize.

Not all programs that a church offers are meant for everyone. A church can also use census data when advertising. Here's an example of three demographic-based segments within a fictitious church:

	Segment 1	Segment 2	Segment 3
Segments	Preschool moms	Single women	Teenagers
Ministries Offered	Women's ministry Preschool ministry Mother's day out	Women's ministry Small groups Missions	Student ministry Missions

Besides age and life stage, there are other means of segmentation. It might be most comfortable to begin with geographical segmentation. Draw concentric circles around the local church at distances of one mile, three miles, and five miles. Then figure out how many people live in those areas around the church, and estimate the drive time and market potential that an area has to be reached by the church. Then segment the church by neighborhood or zip code, depending on your church's overall geographic coverage.

Behavioral segmentation is also beneficial for many churches. Behavioral segmentation involves categorizing people based on what actions have been taken in the past, mainly loyalty, but it could be based on occasions or seasons. For example, you might have a behavioral segment based on those who visit only at Christmas and Easter. You could segment people based on their behavior of opening emails or attending church services regularly.

Psychographic and benefit segmentations are other options. Psychographic segmentation is about how a person sees themselves. This type of segmentation might be beneficial in a new, up-and-coming area. When we started a church in East Nashville, we used the words *trendy, granola,* and *urban* to describe the type of people the church was trying to reach—the kind of people who valued a clean, green space and a dog park.

Benefit segmentation divides people by their felt needs and what the church has to best meet those needs. For example, the church has small groups where people who are lonely and disconnected can connect and begin to build a community. Another example might be burnt-out moms seeking respite, and a church can offer a "mother's day out" for moms of young kids.

Consider starting small when segmenting and grow your segments as your church grows. If your church can choose just three or four components to focus on, that is a spectacular start. You can combine these components into several different types of segments. Using the example of the new church in East Nashville, the area has hipsters who like granola and also businesspeople who want green energy in downtown Nashville. These are two different segments, both being reached by one church.

Before you decide to target a specific segment, it is essential to evaluate if it is worth pursuing specifically by your church, depending on your church's brand, resources, style of worship, and so on. First, identify who is in this segment and if each part requires its own unique marketing mix. Then decide if the segment is substantial enough to be worth pursuing; if your church decides to start a biker ministry and there is only one biker in town, that ministry will not last long. Next, is that segment responsive? Do they react positively to the church's presence in the community? Finally, can the people in this community be reached through community outreach and marketing strategy? The community needs to know that the church exists and understand who the church is and what the church provides to the community in addition to the Sunday worship gathering.

Define Church Verticals

A vertical market is a market where demand originates exclusively from a particular industry or demographic. This is also called a niche market. Companies that implement vertical marketing tactics either create new products aimed at a certain type of consumer, or they modify existing products to make them more appealing to those consumers. Companies that target a particular business vertical are more likely to successfully reach their target customer. In contrast, horizontal marketing tries to appeal to as many different groups of people as possible. A church's verticals are usually specific segments such as children's ministry or student ministry. Most churches already use vertical marketing without knowing what it is called. Each ministry is often known as a marketing vertical with its own goals and needs.

Develop *a persona.* To better clarify a segment for your church, you might want to create a persona. A persona is a fictional representation. You make a specific segment so you can understand them better. For example, Carrie is a single mom at an upper-income level and with a graduate degree. Where would Carrie best be served, and what would Carrie do?

Who are your church's personas? How much do you know about them? Based on data and research, church member personas are fictional representations of your ideal church member—specifically, whom your church is trying to reach. They help you focus your time on prospective guests, guide ministry development to suit your church members' needs, and align all work across your organization, from communication to worship to the sermon.

As a result, you'll be able to reach and retain more guests who come to your church. Having a deep understanding of your church member personas is critical to driving sermon and content creation, ministry development, first-time follow-up, and anything else related to church assimilation and communication.

Personas are critical to your church. But how do you make one? The first step is studying research and congregation data and then representing it within and through your church's communication.

Church member personas help you understand your church members (and prospective church members) better. Personas make it easier for you to tailor your content, messaging, ministry development, and services to meet your target audience's specific needs, behaviors, and concerns.

For example, you may know your target guests are teachers, but do you know their specific needs and interests? What is the background of your ideal church member? It is essential to develop particular personas for your church so you can fully understand what makes your loyal church members tick.

The most vital church member personas start with market research and insights that you gather from your actual church congregation through surveys, interviews, and so on. Depending on your church, you could have a couple of overall church member personas or one for each ministry in your church. However, if you are new to creating personas, start with one or two. You can always develop more personas later if needed.

At their core, personas enable you to personalize or target your communication strategy for different segments of your congregation. Here's how they work: You can send the same emails to everyone in your church's database, or you can segment by persona. Creating segments allows you to custom fit your messaging according to what you know about those different personas.

Here's an example: You have a mother's day out event coming up soon. Should you send this to everyone in your congregation and database, including prospective members? You could, but you might have people who hit the "unsubscribe" button. Instead, use your personas to identify who might want to go to the mother's day out, and create a custom list built around that persona. Would it include all mothers? Perhaps, but probably not, since some mothers might have adult children. Creating personas for your church will help you narrow down exactly what to send to whom and when. They are a valuable portion of the segmentation process.[13]

TARGETING

In targeting, the church is attempting to answer whom the church should try to reach. Of course, we should try to reach all people, but not all people can logically or logistically attend our church. Some people won't like our style of worship, preaching, and so on.

It is best to communicate information about specific church ministries to their appropriate segments. Targeted communication is going to get a better long-term response rate. Email messages based on what a church member has expressed an interest in or needs they have are more relevant and more likely to be read. For example, communicating about the preschool ministry to parents with preschool-aged children is appropriate, but sharing about vacation Bible school with your senior adults might not be the right fit. For them, it could be about volunteering or giving, but it would have to be the right message. Using your congregation's interests, you can now effectively deliver relevant content to them after collecting data about them and creating information from the data that you can use to make the best decisions moving forward.

POSITIONING

The church needs to determine what kind of image it wishes to project in its engaging segments. Positioning ministries as verticals is what market positioning is all about. We do positioning so that potential visitors have a clear, distinct, and desirable understanding of what the church does or represents compared to other churches. "XYZ Baptist

---

[13] For more information on personas, see appendix A.

Church" positions itself as a missions-oriented church that is the first choice for each of its target segments. Its marketing communications stress its core values: its congregation is family-oriented and driven to serve others through mission trips and opportunities.

Positioning is also about clarifying the church's value propositions. I'm a StoryBrand Certified Guide, and I have found that the StoryBrand Framework and process can help a church understand its value propositions quickly. After doing the StoryBrand process with Community Life Church in Navarre, Florida, we determined that their value propositions were community, belonging, and growing in faith. We made sure these were highlighted across their website and communicated frequently in their messaging and communication. Value propositions are the definition of what makes your church unique in your community. For Community Life Church, it was all about community and belonging, which led to growing more Christlike.

For churches to grow, they need to identify their target segments and evaluate each opportunity on a strategic level relative to other churches' strengths in their area. The next step in implementing the church's marketing plan is assigning resources to various ministries and services.

Step 4: Apply the Marketing Mix through the Seven Ps or the 5W1H

We use the Seven Ps as a framework in this strategy, but you can also accomplish the same thing by thinking in terms of 5W1H and answering those questions instead; the process is entirely up to you.

PRODUCT (MINISTRIES, EVENTS, WORSHIP, MISSIONS—WHAT WE DO)

Define the products, ministries, events, and so on with which you will reach your target market or community. What does this ministry do to help reach the church's goals? How does this event support the community's needs outlined in the persona?

Example: Student ministry retreat

PRICE

It is sometimes funny to think of church in terms of price, but there may be a price involved, such as event registration. How much will it cost to do this event? How much will it cost a student to attend camp? Is that cost realistic for the church members' budgets?

Example: The student retreat is $400. Is that realistic for most families in the church?

PLACE

"Location, location, location." We need to think in terms of location. When I worked at Brentwood Baptist Church in Nashville, Tennessee, our church was located right off the interstate. Our pastor, Mike Glenn, included that in our vision, often stating that we were off the interstate because we wanted to send more people out into the world— we were a sending church.

So, in terms of a place for student retreat, the location could play a critical role. Is camp going to be held at a place where students want to go? Is it conducive to the kind of worship environment and experience you are trying to create?

Example: The student retreat will be held at the beach in Panama City, Florida.

PROMOTION

What marketing method will you use to promote this event, ministry, or service? What makes your content unique, apart from the content you already have on your site or social media channels?

Example: We will create TikTok content for our student ministry to increase registrations and help spread the word about the value of the student retreat for students. We will also create Facebook videos explaining the value of the student retreat to parents.

PEOPLE

Who plays a vital role in your church's communication and marketing success? Describe each person's role and how each one contributes to the overall marketing strategy.

Example: Our video producer will work with our student team to develop videos for TikTok and Facebook. Our social media manager will schedule and post the videos to those platforms.

PROCESSES

How will the product be delivered, the event be executed, the ministry be served to your potential visitor or church member? Is it an ongoing service? How will you support their success?

Example: Carrie in marketing will work with Joe in the children's ministry to create videos; then Laura in marketing will email out these videos on a weekly basis.

PHYSICAL EVIDENCE

Where is your ministry? How would visitors produce visible evidence of your church? How will they see physical proof of what happened at camp?

Example: We will have a YouTube channel. We will create video testimonies of what God did at camp through our students.

Step 5: Evaluate Performance Using Marketing Analytics

The final step of the marketing strategy might be the most important: measuring. When we have goals in place across ministries and the church as a whole, we can then measure how effective each ministry is and compare and contrast as goals are met or not met. Understanding the reason for the work, or lack thereof, enables churches to see what areas need improvement. Many people confuse marketing analytics with web analytics, and while web analytics is part of the story of how your church is doing, it does not tell the whole story. Web analytics measures page visits and time on the site (some might also consider church online visits, video views, and social media follows and engagement across those platforms), but marketing analytics is about people and processes. Holistic marketing analytics is about understanding people and processes. For instance, a church may have very different needs for their children's ministry than the senior adult ministry because they serve two completely different groups of people with variable experiences in each area. Therefore, how success in each region is measured will depend entirely on that ministry.

In order to be a successful minister, you have to perform at your best. Performance evaluations can identify problem areas and allow for corrective action in the event that something goes wrong. Why performance was above or below expectations in a certain area should be examined by a senior or executive pastor. If a student minister's performance was below planned levels, was it because the parents weren't involved? Was it because we canceled a certain critical event? Or was it because the leaders involved in setting the objectives were not very good at making estimates? The student minister should only be held accountable for setting unrealistic expectations in their goals.

If you have a small church, and only one minister (or a few) on staff, this same process of evaluating performance can be done by an elder or deacon board.

When we have a holistic view of our marketing across all channels (digital and in-person) and across all our ministries (children, students, and adults), then we can start to truly understand how these multiple channels perform together.

This Is a Guide, Not a Bible

Building a marketing strategy for your church is a guide and not a Bible. Your marketing strategy is something that can change tomorrow, and it very well might need to. This plan might look like it needs to be followed sequentially, but that is not the case—you can move back and forth and make adjustments as needed. For example, you might find your church has a strength that you discovered in the situational analysis that you now want to include in your mission statement. That means your church's mission statement would need to be revised. Either way, going through this process should set your church up for success as you move forward.

Market Research

Market research can help a church leader make the best decision based on data and information. A church leadership team can get this information by gathering, evaluating, and deciphering data from its community and congregation. The research steps are as follows: decide on goals, design research, collect data, interpret the data, and then make marketing decisions based on the new information from that data.[14]

The first step is to decide what kind of information the church is seeking and how it will obtain that information. Does the church's pastor want to build a more prominent church building? Then it would make sense to survey the congregation concerning their thoughts on the matter. It might also make sense to see if more people are moving to the area, which can be done through census data. Define the church's goal for research, then decide how the church will use the resulting information to meet that goal.

---

[14] Grewal and Levy, *Marketing*, 297.

The second step is to design the church's research methodology. What type of data is needed for success in the research project? Does the church need the kind of information that can be obtained via a survey? Does the church need a trusted resource of data like Barna? Then determine the type of research required to get the necessary data, such as surveys, focus groups, observation, interviews, social media, and experiments.

Market researchers generally use two types of data. The first is primary data, which is data the church can obtain on its own, with surveys, focus groups, observation, interviews, social media, and experiments. Using primary data offers a few advantages, such as the ability to be very specific with the questions the church is trying to answer. It can also explain a person's behavior, which is not readily available for secondary data. The disadvantage of attempting to undertake primary research is that it can be expensive, takes time, and usually requires education in properly designing the necessary surveys and collecting data. We will explore primary data in more detail shortly.

Secondary data is the research an organization might seek out by searching online or in books, and it is typically already done by someone else. Barna Research and Pew Research Center are known for creating and providing excellent secondary research. Other secondary research examples include syndicated sources (like Nielsen), academic journals, books, Internet information from trusted sources, and census data. Most marketing research books would also include sales invoices from the company as a form of secondary data. In that same way, plan on using giving statements and attendance records. One advantage of secondary research is that it is sometimes available for free or very inexpensively, excluding syndicated data. Secondary research also saves time because it is already available, and the church does not have to go through the stage of designing the study.

If the church is looking for demographic data on a given community, check out these resources: the Urban Institute, which has interactive maps on schools, housing, and education; the US Census Bureau at http://data.census.gov, which allows search by zip code to find a specific area's ethnicities, ages, income levels, and other social demographics; and state and local government websites, including local libraries.

Primary data can fall into two categories: quantitative or qualitative. Qualitative data includes observation, in-depth interviews, focus groups, and even social media. Observation is what it sounds like: watching people. We already do this for attendance in most churches, but now many cameras have technology that can count how many people enter a building and their interaction once inside. Will churches start using this kind of "invasive observation" technology? It remains to be seen.

Social media is another form of qualitative data. We can compare our church's page to that of other churches nearby. We can also create virtual communities for our church such as a Facebook Group (discussed in chapter 4 on social media) and gather information in those communities with informal polling. Churches can also use sentiment analysis to see how users feel about their church by analyzing comments that people make about the church online.

Qualitative data can also be obtained through interviews and focus groups. These are the most costly and time-consuming but can be extremely beneficial. Interviews are typically done one-on-one with a trained researcher. Focus groups are generally small groups of people with a trained facilitator, typically less structured than interviews, and seeking more qualitative data. Focus groups could be beneficial for either a new or an older church that is trying to determine how people in the area come to know of their church and how they feel about that church in particular.

Comparatively, quantitative data includes experiments, surveys, scanner data, and panel data. Most churches use qualitative data and some methods of quantitative data like surveys.

The third step in research is to collect the data from the research. The church would typically receive secondary data before making decisions based on the research. Primary research would only be collected to address particular concerns and specific needs in the study. For example, the church could survey about communication preferences. The survey included in appendix C demonstrates a good way to find out how, when, and how often the congregation likes to communicate with the leaders of the church. The results of this survey might surprise most churches. Surveying the community is a critical practice that the church should do annually.

The fourth step is to turn all this data into information. Data is just raw information like spreadsheets upon spreadsheets. It is challenging to quickly gather what a spreadsheet is conveying, so we must turn the raw data into information. Information is data that has been explained or interpreted. Market researchers often take results from their research and turn them into charts and graphs to describe the data quickly and efficiently so that leaders can make decisions more effectively. Look at the chart below. Is it possible to immediately infer which church is better overall from the data? Can the safer one be found quickly? Which one is cleaner? Which one has more programs? Which one is more accessible? Church leaders can take what they want from this information. Many will say they do not wish to be the cleanest church, just the safest, and so on.

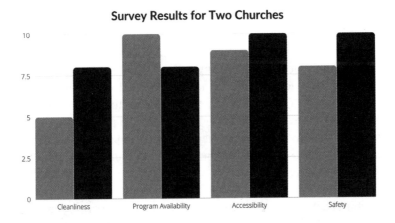

Survey Results for Two Churches

Finally, the last step is to move research into action by creating a plan of what the church will now do with this information. Completing the research process is only meaningful if that research leads to change. It is essential to compile research into a report with the church's findings, how the church gathered the data, what information was collected, and what conclusions the church came to going forward.

Big Data

"Big Data" incorporates multiple data points from phones, computers, watches, smart televisions, cameras, and more to compile a bigger picture of who we are as consumers and persons. Big Data is changing the church. However, whether Big Data is a force for good or evil depends on how it is used.

Big Data can be scary, but it can also be beneficial. We as church leaders now have access to more data *about* more data than ever before. Having this data is great news when it comes to sharing the gospel. Never before has the church had access to more information about the people in our communities. There are a few Christian companies that are researching Big Data, for example Gloo.

What are some of the benefits of Big Data for the church? First, Big Data can be used to fundraise more effectively. Church leaders have been slow to adopt Big Data technology, but they're finally realizing this new technology can provide more information and knowledge on who, when, and why people donate.

Big Data can also give insights into the demographics of a church community and how it is changing over time. This information allows churches to make more informed decisions about current outreach efforts, building renovations, staffing changes, and so on that will help them better cater to those in attendance while also looking ahead to future needs. Big Data makes it possible for pastors of any size congregation or in any denomination to use this technology, not just because they want to but because they need to use it if they are going to keep up with trends both within their faith communities and their local community at large.

There are things to consider when choosing to use Big Data at your church: Who has access to the data? Who has permission to use Big Data? What's happening with this information after the user is done with it? From the pastor to staff and volunteers, Big Data has become an integral part of how churches operate. But before engaging in any church-related activities involving this form of analytics, it's important to consider privacy concerns, technical knowledge, and skill sets required for handling these datasets, as well as who has permission to access them. Ultimately, the church needs to be aware of the risks and benefits of using Big Data for it to be a force for good.

Chapter 2:

Branding

Why Is Branding Important?

"Brands are one of the most valuable yet least understood of assets."[1]

Everyone loves a good story. Whether it is reading a novel, watching a movie, or calling a friend, we innately love stories. Throughout history, there have been many amazing storytellers such as Shakespeare, Mark Twain, Harper Lee, and my personal favorite, J. K. Rowling. One storyteller who does not often make the list is Jesus.

One thing we know for sure is that Jesus was quite the storyteller. Often, when Jesus was asked a question, instead of answering the question directly, he launched into a story. Not only did Jesus choose to use stories, but he used stories that challenged the status quo. For example, the idea of loving your neighbor as yourself is foundational in most churches, but when Jesus taught this point, he did not just state, "Treat others as you want to be treated." Instead, he told a story.

---

[1] ISO, "Brand Evaluation—Principles and Fundamentals," ISO, accessed September 23, 2021, https://www.iso.org/obp/ui/#iso:std:iso:20671:dis:ed-1:v1:en.

You probably remember the story of the Good Samaritan. This story would have been considered one of Jesus's most controversial at the time. For context, Jews hated Samaritans. A Samaritan helping a Jew in Jesus's day would have left everyone stunned. We are introduced to a Jewish man who has been beaten and abandoned by robbers and is lying on the side of the road close to death. A Jew and a non-Jew ignored him twice, and then the Samaritan helped him.

Stories help build major brands. Everyone knows the story about Steve Jobs and Apple or Bill Gates and Microsoft. Businesses live and die based on their branding, but what about churches? It is not so easy to say. It is not as quantifiable, but branding plays a vital role in the church regardless. Branding can help us find out a lot about a church—its worship style, its beliefs, its denomination. It can unite us, and sometimes it can divide us. There's no doubt that branding plays an essential role in the church. Your job as a church communicator is to create, protect, and serve the church's brand. No one else will care about the brand or protect the brand as much as you will.

Branding is also essential because short-term memory is limited. Susan Weinschenk notes, "There's only so much people can hold in working memory before they forget it."[2] Donald Miller says in *Building a StoryBrand,* "So what do customers [people] do when we blast a bunch of noise [information] at them? They ignore us."[3] He goes on to say, "The first mistake brands make is they fail to focus on the aspects of their offer that will help people survive and thrive."[4]

It is essential to use other information to help your brand stick. Although branding is much more than a logo, logos are important, and generally most people only associate a brand with its logo. What are some ways to help a church's brand stick? The best way to help a brand become "sticky" is through telling a story. Jesus is an excellent example of this. He used parables (teaching stories) to help people remember the message he was trying to teach.

"Never judge a book by its cover." Whoever said this has never browsed a bookstore. With so many choices in a bookstore, almost the only way to judge a book is by its cover.

---

[2] Susan Weinschenk, *100 Things Every Designer Needs to Know about People* (San Francisco: New Riders, 2020), 46–47.

[3] Miller, *Building a StoryBrand,* 7 (see chap. 1, n. 3).

[4] Miller, 7.

The same goes for churches; there are so many of them that sometimes the only way to judge them is by their cover—their brand, their name, and often their buildings.

Weinschenk asks, "How do people move things from working memory into long-term memory? There are basically two ways: repeat it a lot or connect it to something they already know."[5] How can this be applied to churches? We should carry our branding through to every piece of printed, digital, and video media that we have. We should state our mission often. And we should connect our mission, vision, and brand to something people already know and love about us. Many churches base their logos on a historical landmark or actual physical asset of their church. For example, Brentwood Baptist Church's logo is based on an intricate window design, and First Mt. Juliet based their logo on a cross design that is located prominently in their baptistery.

Branding also provides a way to differentiate from competitors, or in this case, other churches or denominations. Both Assemblies of God and Baptists are church denominations, but they provide different styles of worship and teaching. Seekers looking for a church might decide they care more for one than the other.

Before we go any further, let us answer these questions from my friend Brandon Cox, a former pastor and church expert, about branding:

- What story do we want people to associate with our church? How would we like people to feel when they think about us?
- What story do people tell about us? And how do we know this?
- Does the appearance of our building, landscaping, and outdoor signage communicate the feelings we want people to experience?
- Do we have a church logo that communicates the feeling and the story we want people to experience?
- Do our website, bulletin, and other printed materials such as brochures, business or invitation cards, or postcards uniformly agree with the story we're telling across the board?[6]

A 2006 CBS News article states, "Walker-Smith says we've gone from being exposed to about 500 ads a day back in the 1970s to as

---

[5] Weinschenk, *100 Things Every Designer Needs to Know*, 46.

[6] Brandon Cox, "33 Questions for Auditing Your Church's Social Media Effectiveness," Pastor Brandon Cox, February 4, 2015, https://brandonacox.com/dare-audit-churchs -communication-strategy-33-questions-ask.

many as 5,000 a day today."[7] The church must speak to consumers in a way that stands out among the 5,000 commercial messages they are bombarded with every day.

What Is Branding?

Here's one definition of *branding:* "A brand is a name, term, design, symbol or any other feature that identifies one seller's good or service as distinct from those of other sellers."[8] In your community, your church has a brand. What can a church do to focus on visual messages that make up its brand identity?

Logos, and brands by extension, are defined by giving careful attention to detail. Branding, however, is more than a logo. Logos are a part of branding, but branding is all-encompassing. Branding includes the brand name, URLs, characters, slogans or taglines, jingles, sounds, and, for many churches, a denominational name. Strong brands are rarely the result of one person's ideas but rather a mix of creative input from many people along with the church's goals.

Branding is an asset. Most brands are worth actual money; a church brand is no different. To understand a local church's brand, it is important to know what people say about the church when they talk about it within the community. Many businesses and churches often make the mistake of thinking a brand is just a logo. Branding means bringing the messaging, the mission, the vision, the look, and who you are all under one umbrella. It is important that branding is cohesive and tells one overarching clear and compelling story about who you are and what you are doing.

It is very easy for a church's brand message to get lost in translation in the church itself. Branding and messaging can be difficult to clarify within a congregation or community. What are you doing that is confusing to potential future members? How can you help people seeking your church get connected easily? All those questions are answered by good branding and clear messaging.

Before we go on, it is important to understand all the parts of a brand. There is a brand name, which is the most commonly known

---

[7] Caitlin Johnson, "Cutting through Advertising Clutter," CBS News, September 17, 2006, https://www.cbsnews.com/news/cutting-through-advertising-clutter.

[8] "Brand," Common Language Marketing Dictionary, accessed September 23, 2021, https://marketing-dictionary.org/b/brand.

portion of any brand, and it is usually what is spoken. For example, Brentwood Baptist Church conveys a certain brand image. Next would be logos, which is what most people think of when they think of a brand. Most people tend to think of the brand name and the logo and not much else, but there's a lot more to a brand than that.

The brand might also have a tagline or slogan like, "Connecting People with Jesus Christ." Sometimes a brand has a character, like Tony the Tiger from Frosted Flakes, or a biblical character might be drawn upon for a children's ministry. Finally, the church's URL is also part of the brand. Many times, the URL that a church wants is already taken, but with the rise of new top-level domain names like dot church (.church), there are a lot more options today.

Brand Names: Naming Your Church

"Church names are like tattoos—you better love it because you'll have it until you are seventy."
—Chad Brooks, The Foundry, West Monroe, Louisiana

Church names are like tattoos. Just like tattoos, you have to

- decide you can live with it for a long time,
- love it and identify with it, and
- know it is hard to remove or change.

Life. Point. Cross. Way. Harvest. Fields. Church. What's in a church name? The first consideration should be the community. What are its expectations? Do we want to feed into those expectations, or do we wish to defy them? The next question is: Do we want to use our denominational nomenclature in our church name, and how important is it that we do? There also needs to be a consideration for common names so that there is no confusion between two churches with similar-sounding names but different affiliations. Names remain a crucial part of church branding and church planting.

History of Church Naming

Since the beginning of Christianity, churches were mostly named after geographic areas or major landmarks, but somewhere along the way, this changed. The historical backdrop of church naming is intricate. Denominations were formed mostly after the Reformation. Before the

Reformation, there were two primary branches of Christianity: Roman Catholic and Eastern Orthodox. Groups inside those have existed since before the Reformation, although not in a denominational sense that we mean today.

In recent history, the church has adopted an area strategy. There would be a Baptist, Methodist, Presbyterian, Catholic, and other assembly for every parish or area. Its location would generally be its name, along with its denomination—for example, Clanton United Methodist Church, Clanton Assemblies of God, and so forth. Parish churches were then settled within walking distances of communities. Things started to change as portability expanded and mobility increased, which is why churches expanded after World War II. Names began to move to road names, geographic landmark names, or more specialty names, still attached to the location. Church naming has changed substantially in the last fifty years, and many have lost their denominational nomenclature.

Four Types of Church Brand Names

Naming your church comes with some flexibility. Let's look at four different naming conventions.

1. *Geographic names*: This is the most common naming convention for a church. It sometimes also includes the denomination, but that has fallen out of style in the last forty years (see the section "Including the Denomination in Your Church's Name"). Classically done, this is "Your City Church," like "Birmingham Church," but it also includes variations like "Birmingham City Church," "The Church in Birmingham," "The Church at Birmingham," and so on.

2. *Historical or theological names:* Sometimes churches are named after something found in history that relates to the church or relates to something specific in Scripture that has inspired the church body. An example of this would be the "Foundry" church: "John Wesley's headquarters in London were, by chance, called the Foundry. The name might have been invented for him, for he was a sort of itinerant furnace of energy. Clocking up more than 200,000 miles by horse and

foot by his mid-80s, he explained his untiring health by the habit of getting up daily at 4am and preaching at five."[9]

3. *Christian "pendant" names:* These names include things like "Cross," "Grace," "Life," "Redemption," "Redeemer," "Harvest," and many variations of these.

4. *Noun/verb names:* These are not usually specific to a geographic area, but they resonate because of a feeling of inspiration that is drawn on from the pastors, elders, or congregation. These include but are not limited to phrases and names like, "Elevation," "Rise," "Awaken," "Vibe," and so on.[10]

Naming a church takes discernment, discussion, and prayer. Have you ever named a church? What church do you attend now? How did they come by their name?

Including the Denomination in Your Church's Name

What was the first church to use their denomination's name in their church name? What was the first to drop their denominational name in recent memory? Do denominational names matter? Many churches still use a denominational name in their church's name. However, more recently, many churches are choosing not to include the denomination for several reasons.

A pastor in my Church Communications Facebook Group, Dan Sweaza, has said of denominational naming, "Religions disagree on primary issues. Denominations disagree on secondary (and tertiary) issues. Why highlight secondary issues at the most introductory level? Do you know who knows the difference between Baptist churches and Pentecostal churches? Christians. Do you know who does not? Non-believers."[11]

Churches have long used denominational names to associate with a certain set of beliefs. Let's do a little research about denominational names today. Every year, *Outreach Magazine,* along with Lifeway

---

[9] Christopher Howse, "A Furnace of Energy Whose Sermons Attracted Thousands," Telegraph Media Group, June 16, 2003, https://www.telegraph.co.uk/news/uknews/1433117/A-furnace-of-energy-whose-sermons-attracted-thousands.html.

[10] For a bit of fun poking at church names, you can visit https://namemy.church/, which will generate a random name with every refresh. It is a very fun tool but not to be taken seriously.

[11] Dan Sweaza, "Church Communications Facebook Group," Facebook, accessed March 15, 2021, https://www.facebook.com/groups/churchcomm/permalink/1499869570196636.

Research, compiles a list of the fastest-growing churches and the largest churches in America. Using this list, and only noting the Southern Baptist Convention (SBC) churches, let us take a look at their names.

THE FASTEST GROWING CHURCHES OF 2019 (SBC ONLY)

Information from BPNews.net in 2019 cited the fastest-growing churches in the Southern Baptist denomination. In the following list notice their naming convention: Mercy Hill, 5 Point Church, Sandals Church, Venture Church, Rolling Hills Community Church, Battle Creek Church, River Oak Church, First Baptist Jackson, Bethlehem Church, Brentwood Baptist Church, Second Baptist Church, Cascade Hills Church, Lifepoint Church, Brookwood Church, First Baptist Church of Bryan, Central Baptist Church, and Chets Creek Church.[12]

Out of the 100 fastest growing churches in the United States, seventeen are SBC. Looking at their names, only five out of the seventeen churches, or less than half, include "Baptist" in their names. If we look into their history, we can assume that the five churches in the fastest-growing list are also somewhat older churches, with most being founded well before the 1980s—First Baptist Jackson, Mississippi, founded 1838;[13] Brentwood Baptist Church, Brentwood, Tennessee, founded 1969;[14] Second Baptist Church, Conway, Arkansas, founded 1922;[15] First Baptist Church, Bryan, Texas, founded 1866;[16] and Central Baptist Church, Jonesboro, Arkansas, founded 1931.[17] How many churches do you know that use their denomination as part of their name? Are they older congregations? Younger? What trends do you currently see in church naming?

---

[12] Diana Chandler, "Fastest-Growing, Largest Churches: Who Made the List?," Baptist Press, September 12, 2019, https://www.baptistpress.com/resource-library/news/fastest-growing-largest-churches-who-made-the-list.

[13] "Our Story: First Baptist Jackson," First Baptist Jackson, accessed March 19, 2021, https://www.firstbaptistjackson.org/our-story.

[14] "History," Brentwood Baptist, accessed March 17, 2021, https://brentwoodbaptist.com/about/history.

[15] "Second Baptist Church," Outreach 100, accessed March 19, 2021, https://outreach100.com/churches/second-baptist-church-1.

[16] "First Baptist Bryan," *Outreach Magazine*, June 26, 2019, https://outreachmagazine.com/church/first-baptist-bryan.

[17] "Our Story," Central Baptist, accessed March 19, 2021, https://centralbaptist.com/ourstory.

How to Name a Church

Naming a church is a complicated process. When studying past naming conventions, we find what has worked well in the past might not work well in the future, because people are more nomadic than ever before. Would a church by any other name reach as many people as possible in a given community?

TYPICAL CHURCH NAMES

The past thirty years have seen churches shift away from names that are overtly "churchy." The questions to ask are:

* Do we want to include "church" in the name at all?
* Do we want the church name to sound like a typical church name?

There's absolutely nothing wrong with naming your church something typical. In recent years, churches were into calling their churches something hip like The Loft, and that is also an option. But when people are learning about Christianity, they look for the word *church* online. Therefore, having a "church" name is not bad (even if it is not entirely trendy) because at least people far from Christ will recognize immediately that this is a church and not a cult. An example of a conventional church name might be "Jackson Baptist Church" or "Jackson Church," using the location and the word church to name it.

LOCATION-BASED NAMES

Here are some additional questions to ask when considering whether to base a church name on location:

* Do we want to include the location in the church name?
* Are we planning on expanding to other cities?
* Do we plan on reaching people in other towns through the original church and campus?
* Are there any negative connotations associated with our town?

There are many advantages to naming a church with the location:

1. Google will love it because Google loves local places with logical names, so LOCATION + CHURCH will help the church rise in the search ranks.
2. It can create a sense of community in the local area.

3. It might also help distinguish the church from other churches if they are all using different names.

There are also some disadvantages:

1. A location-based name can constrain a church as it grows and moves or relocates in the future. That means an immediate rebrand would have to follow.
2. Having a church of one town meet in another town might be confusing and stop people from associating with that town.

VISIONARY OR CHRISTIAN-WORD NAMES

Many churches get their names because of a vision the pastor has for the church. There are also many churches named from a Greek or Hebrew word. A word of caution in naming your church after these things: there's a high probability that people encountering a church, or even church in general for the first time, will not understand the purpose of a name like that. Any name requiring explanation runs the risk of being confusing, obscure, or even cheesy to those who hear it for the first time without the context.

When your church chooses a name, it is essential for it to be clear and communicate a vital priority. An example such as "Living Hope Church" is both visionary and self-explanatory.[18]

Brand Extensions: Naming the Ministries of Your Church

It cannot be stressed enough that ministry names should be clear, not cute. This is important not only for longevity purposes but also because the church will become a "house of brands" rather than a "branded house."

For example, you are looking for a name for your church's women's ministry. If your church's name is Calvary, go with "Calvary Women's Ministry." The same is true with student ministries, children's ministries, and so on. It is easy to think a catchy name will attract more people. It will not. Give it a name that visitors and members alike will recognize as what it is, even if they have never heard it before. Clever names will cause you to miss out on many ministry

---

[18] For more information on church naming, see appendix D.

opportunities because people will not recognize what the ministry is and will simply not attend or seek out further information.

Youth Specialties came up with a list of some questions to ask before deciding to name ministries or programs:

1. Does your ministry/program need a name?
2. Should it match the church's name?
3. What name will make sense?
4. What name will make it unique?
5. What name will have longevity?
6. What name will give you flexibility?[19]

HOUSE OF BRANDS VS. BRANDED HOUSE

Naming ministries is not unlike naming a church. You will often have to stick with it for a long time and commit. Let's consider the argument again for a house of brands versus a branded house. See the example below of the house of brands used by Saraland Baptist Church. Saraland Baptist Church has a Next Gen ministry, but what does that mean to an outsider? I'm not so sure they would figure it out. Inside that Next Gen ministry is Explode Youth, which sounds kind of dangerous. Then we have Little Stars and Tiny Tots. Again, there's not much clarity as to what those ministries are or what they do. The same could be said for Gospel Communities and its subgroups as well as Empower Ministries. A visitor attending the church for the very first time might feel confused or left out by all this insider language or jargon. Additionally, maintaining these brands in the long term can be difficult.

The chart on the next page shows Saraland Baptist as a house of brands. They have several unique, individual brands beneath their main brand, Saraland Baptist. Each of these brands is distinctive and has a life of its own, including its own logo, brand voice, style guide, and so on. This creates more work for the brand director, who must oversee that all these brands do not overlap or create competition with themselves and that they all have their own unique selling proposition and their own positioning in the marketing strategy.

---

[19] Steve Cullum, "6 Questions to Ask as You Are Naming Ministries/Programs," *YS Blog,* March 30, 2020, https://blog.youthspecialties.com/6-questions-to-ask-as-you-are-naming-ministries-programs.

House of Brands

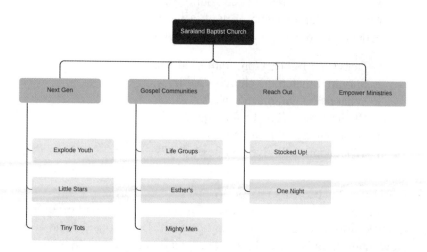

Many churches, especially during the '90s, were a house of brands. When I was growing up my home church, Mulberry Baptist Church, had Little Stars for children, Youth for students, and Forever Young for senior adults. Each of these phrases was very internally focused, and an outsider might be confused about what all these ministries meant. There was no explanation provided in any printed materials. Basically, the only way to know was through word of mouth and just being there for a while.

Instead, I recommend becoming a branded house. A branded house is a company that creates different products but all under the same name. A branded house consists of brand extensions, or sub-brands, that do not deter from the main brand. This builds a more recognizable, sustainable brand and, therefore, a stronger brand overall.

Look again at Saraland Baptist Church. The chart on the next page shows how Saraland Baptist Church might look as a branded house: it has several brand extensions—Saraland Family Ministry, Saraland Discipleship, Saraland Missions, and Saraland Special Needs. All of these brands fall under Saraland Baptist Church. They all carry the Saraland name; they just extend its use. A branded house can extend a church's brand name in a useful way that is clear to the people visiting the church. Again, we want to be clear, not cute.

Branded House

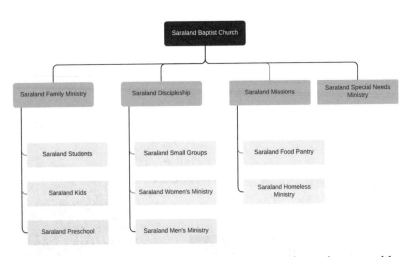

There is a possibility of rebranding happening when an older church is merged with a newer church as a revitalization process. During that time, those congregations will need to determine the best course of action to move forward with their branding messages and ask themselves the following questions: Should they stay distinctive? Should they co-brand? Should they be totally assimilated and become a branded house like the "mother church"?

Brand extensions can be incredibly helpful when done correctly. It is important to weigh the advantages and disadvantages of naming new programs and ministries at your church. Whether you are a branded house or a house of brands will determine how your branding strategy works in the future and how your community perceives your church. Being as clear as possible about your ministries when naming will help avoid some confusion.

Logos

Logos are the most basic form of branding. A logo is a company's or church's visual identity simplified into an icon usually accompanying a wordmark of some kind. A logo helps people easily identify and choose between products, services, and, yes, even churches. The following five elements go into creating a great logo design:

1. Simple
2. Timeless
3. Versatile
4. Unique
5. Memorable

HARVEST CHURCH

From the color scheme to the logo and everything in between, Harvest Church is a great example of what consistent branding can look like.[20] The logo is rather intricate but made simplistic by factors such as the color scheme, placement, and sizing. The logo itself is one that is timeless in the sense

that it is clean and simple. It can be used for many different purposes, including generational aspects of a church's congregation.

The colors are neutral as well, so over the course of time, if the church changes its branding color scheme, the logo itself can still be recognizable and constant through any changes that might occur. The logo is versatile because it can match virtually anything and be used in multiple media—watermarks, graphics, print media, you name it. Whether a logo stands alone or with the name of different ministries, it must be recognizable.

A good product example of this is Nike. Any time someone sees a swoosh, regardless of whether the name Nike is on the product, it is automatically registered in a consumer's brain as Nike. A logo should lend itself to quick recognition and memorability. A logo should not only be able to stand alone, but it should be able to stand out. A church's branding is only as strong as its design. As the communications team, you hold the ability to form the vision of your church through your visitors' and members' eyes. The final goal of a logo is

---

[20] Permission for use granted by Benjamin Oberemok of Harvest Church via email, March 9, 2021.

to bring consistency throughout the branding of a church. Consistency conveys and increases credibility with your audience.

WAYPOINT

A classic play on words in logo form is shown in Waypoint Church's logo.[21] Talk about simple and timeless! The simplicity and minimalistic nature of an arrow cuts through all the marketing noise you see in the field these days. This logo is timeless because no

one will ever have a question about what it is or why it is there—whether someone sees it tomorrow or 200 years from now. It will always be a recognizable symbol, and the meaning will always be understood. Now, just because you use a symbol that is timeless does not guarantee its memorability.

Adding a little flair to the logo is what brands it as Waypoint Church. The arrow can be used anywhere—on any print piece or graphic—and it will be recognizable as Waypoint. The versatility that comes with a clean

[21] https://waypointchurch.com/. Permission for use granted by Ryan Weiss of WayPoint Church via email, March 18, 2021.

logo enhances the branding possibilities and capabilities of a church. Do not assume that just because a logo is simple, it cannot be unique.

A logo encompasses the brand, company, business, church, or wherever you are working. You hold the capability of framing a logo in whatever light you choose. Branding a logo is so much more than the symbol. What colors surround it? How does it blend with the name, identity, design, and character of the church? How does the logo fit into other things your church is doing? Does it complement or distract from the message? Thinking through the identity of the church will clear up any questions about the direction a logo needs to take. If the identity of the church is too unclear to create a logo around, it is time to back up and reevaluate what the church values.

Canvas Church[22]

Canvas Church's logo is a textbook example of simple yet impactful. In any aspect of the church—social media, print media, or anything in between—you will see the color orange or the blank canvas with the orange outline (their logo). It is incredibly simple and timeless, but as a consumer of media, anytime I
see the color orange I immediately think "Canvas Church." Here's the ingenious idea of that branding color and logo: even if it is not Canvas Church that has posted, I still think of them, and nine times out of ten I'll go and search their account (Instagram: @canvas_fl) to see any new creative posts they have made or news about the church—and I do not even attend Canvas. Despite that, I hold a stake of interest in that church simply because their logo and branding are so intentional.

Additionally, their logo is extremely versatile. Whether it is on the side of the building, inside the welcome center, or on their shirts, giveaways, print media, or digital media, it is everywhere, and it doesn't distract from anything else in that same creative space. The message is still delivered, with their logo complementing the purpose. It is unique and memorable because the logo has a storytelling capability.

Consumers are drawn to storytelling in advertising; when businesses are weighing whether they should do a logical or emotional advertisement, they often lean toward emotional because that is what connects with consumer buying habits. It is no different when it comes

---

[22] https://www.canvasfl.com. Permission for use granted by Austin Pluskot of Canvas Church via email, March 18, 2021.

to church branding and logos. Of course, you are not getting someone to buy a product from a church, but you are trying to get them in your doors to experience the gospel and the environment. There is more on storytelling in chapter 7 on public relations.

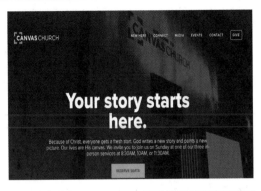

Canvas Church's name was inspired by Eph 2:10: "For we are God's masterpiece" (NLT). Canvas Church believes that we are God's canvas, where he creates something uniquely beautiful as we pursue a life with him. Scripture is brought out through a logo, and the storytelling behind it makes it incredibly memorable.

Rebranding

There comes a point in the life of any church when the thought of rebranding crosses a church leader's mind. Rebranding usually happens for a number of

reasons. Because many churches are named for their geography and denomination, some churches find this limits them as they continue to grow. Many churches plant campuses and other churches, so the geographic name does not make sense because they are no longer just in that location. Some find the denominational nomenclature limits their reach in a certain community.

There are also a lot of emotions that weigh in to rebranding. There will likely be many longtime members who feel a sense of pride and recognition with the name of the church as it is. This is especially true in an older church with an older congregation. The church leader should consider if it is best to keep the name or count the cost— especially if the costs are detrimental to growth.

When naming a church, it is important to think about the story that names tell. With a typical geographical and denominational name, church leaders do not get the chance to craft a brand story with their name. But when it comes to naming a church more creatively, the church has more freedom to craft a beautiful narrative that allows it to share the gospel and the story of the church.

We previously learned about creating a branded house versus a house of brands. I have found churches that sought to become branded houses after some time of being a house of brands. For example, Central Peninsula Church used to be a house of brands. Each ministry had its own distinct logo and feel associated with it.[23]

When Central Peninsula Church became a branded house, their brand became much more communicative and easier for the viewer to understand.

When considering rebranding, you should ask yourself several questions:

1. Why do you personally feel the church needs to be rebranded?
2. Are you embarrassed by your current branding? What parts of it

---

[23] Permission for use granted by Sandy Hughes of Central Peninsula Church via email, March 8, 2021.

embarrass you? The name? The logo? The tagline?

3. Who is your target audience? Has that changed since the original branding was developed?
4. Have the mission and vision changed? If so, in what way?
5. Are you seeking a name change? Will ministries' names change?
6. Who needs to be at the table when making these decisions?
7. Are you going to seek outside help during your rebranding?
8. Has it been some time (more than two years) since your last refresh?

Because branding consists of many parts, more than just a logo needs to be considered. For example, there's a name, URL, and so on. That is determinative of which parts need to be rebranded and which do not. You might find that your church name is fine, but your logo has suffered from a design fad. You might find your church name no longer represents who you are because your geographical location has changed. Whatever the reason, be sure to move forward with clarity, and create a plan. Write down all the places that the current brand exists—the website, the signage, the church building, the business cards, and so forth—make a plan of replacement for those items, and budget for it.

While rebranding, remember the old adage: "Keep it short and simple." Creating branding that speaks clarity rather than confusion will help your church succeed.

Developing a Brand Voice

A church's brand voice is the church's personality, as seen through its communications and marketing efforts. Churches should reflect their values and beliefs in their tone of voice. A formal tone can be used for sermons, announcements, or other formal occasions. An informal tone of voice can be used to communicate online.

First, determine the church's branding voice. The branding voice should be directly related to the church's mission statement. Choose words and statements carefully and deliberately. Second, determine the tone of voice the church wants to use with its target audience (formal, informal, playful, or serious). Finally, write or speak with consistency in the church's brand voice. For church members, it is helpful to communicate these guidelines in a style guide or through an informational brochure that is used to promote the church's ministry, beliefs, values, and programs.

Chapter 3

Digital Marketing

What Is Digital Marketing?

Digital marketing has changed the very definition of marketing over the last twenty years. It encompasses all digital strategies, including social media, video content, content marketing, emailing, texting, search engines, and websites. Essentially, digital marketing involves anything and everything you can do on your phone or computer and how marketers can reach that audience where they are—online. Social media, email, and other channels are all part of digital marketing.

According to Pew Research, "about three-in-ten U.S. adults say they are 'almost constantly' online."[1] That same research states that roughly eight in ten American adults go online at least daily, multiple times per day. Thus, digital marketing has never been as essential to success as it is today in the online marketplace and for the church. Churches can take advantage of digital marketing to reach their

---

[1] Andrew Perrin and Sara Atske, "About Three-in-Ten U.S. Adults Say They Are 'Almost Constantly' Online," Pew Research Center, updated March 26, 2021, https://www.pewresearch.org/fact-tank/2019/07/25/americans-going-online-almost-constantly.

communities and spread the word about what they stand for, particularly for church leaders who want people who are not regular churchgoers to begin to attend regularly.

Digital marketing includes anything done over the Internet, including search engine optimization (SEO) tactics using keywords, metadata tags, social media networks, and websites. Digitalization has taken place in the church. More people are coming to the church because of marketers who use social media platforms such as Facebook or Instagram. New residents can be connected with churches through social media platforms that they use on their smartphones, like Yelp and LinkedIn. Social media marketing is an effective form of outreach for churches where word-of-mouth advertising once reigned supreme.

Why Digital Marketing Matters

When you are searching for a new lawn care company, where do you go? When you are searching for a new church, where do you go? Most people would start their search on Google. "Google" has become synonymous with "search" in the last few decades. It is where the beginning and end of searches will happen for most people.

But the question is, where would your church land when people searched for it? How will they find you? Will they only find a map of how to get to you? Or will they find reviews, photos, your website brimming with articles about life change, practical guides on prayer, and how to receive salvation? The answer depends on your digital marketing strategy.

Digital marketing matters because people are connecting online. Every day meaningful relationships start on the Internet. The Internet has definitely evolved from the *You've Got Mail* days to a very advanced form of communication that encompasses business and personal contact and connection.

Many people connect online because of common interests. This happened to me as a child. It is every parent's worst nightmare, but I connected with thousands of people through Internet forums about Harry Potter. There were not many people my age at that time reading Harry Potter in my local area, and I wanted to connect with others, so I sought out online forums to fill that need to connect with other people. I soon found and created my own community online, which is why I am so passionate about using digital marketing tactics to reach people for the gospel. If I can accidentally on purpose create meaningful relationships online and share the gospel in those online relationships as a child in 1999, I'm convinced the church can too.

Digital marketing helps us connect with people where they are online, often in what they are already doing or interested in. What I love about digital marketing in comparison to print advertising or commercial advertising is that it is more of a pull strategy than a push. With digital marketing, we usually are not interrupting their favorite show with a commercial or showing a billboard with an indirect message about Sunday worship on someone's drive to work. We are intentionally targeting those we want to reach without interrupting. We are pulling people to our church through our intentional online efforts by creating content that is irresistible and actually helpful to our community.

Google Your Church

Take a moment and Google your church now. What's there? Do you have decent reviews? Do you have photos? Does Google have a link to your website? The first step to making your Google presence better is by reviewing it, or auditing it, and comparing it to other churches in the area. The list that shows with a map at the top of Google is known as Google Local Pack on the Search Engine Results Page (SERP). Is your church far down the list when you search for "churches near me"? Compare and take note of other churches' Google listings. Besides the map, you can view pictures, office hours, the call button, and website address.

Now that you have done your own audit of your Google Local Pack presence, how can we make it better? You should first claim your Google My Business listing. If you haven't done that, it is really easy. First, search for your church in Google, click on your church, and then click "Own this business?" I recommend you do this on your church's Google account so it is easy to find for the next person. Then you will have to verify that you do in fact "own this business."

Verifying ownership of a business listing can be done instantly through a phone call, or it could take a couple of weeks by sending a postcard. For some churches, the only time they needed to claim their business listing was because they needed to update their address or phone number. If you have already moved addresses or telephone numbers, it can be tricky, so I recommend you do this earlier rather than later when you really have to update. Another way to verify ownership is through Google Analytics if the church's website is set up with it and is already the same website on the listing itself. You would need to use the same Gmail account you used previously in Google Analytics.

Update the church's Google My Business listing often to improve its Local Pack ranking on Google. Ensure that the business name, or church name in this case, is correct. Be sure that the category of the business is "church"; there may even be a more specific listing for a denomination like "Baptist Church." Go line by line in the "About" information, often referred to as NAP data (Name, Address, Phone), to make sure the information is current. Make changes to the hours listed and update the web address as needed.

After updating the basic information, the next step is to upload photography. Pictures are an important part of choosing a church. Do the pictures represent people who look like me? Be sure to include diversity if the church is diverse. Be careful uploading pictures of children; either ask a photographer to avoid children, or be sure to have a media release form signed by a parent or guardian. Additionally, it is recommended that the church communicator takes 360° photos of the church's building and exterior. This can be done on a smartphone with the app Google Street View. Be sure to include relevant photos from each ministry and to upload new photos often.

Your Google My Business listing may also include citations from Yelp or the Yellow Pages. If you have not claimed your listings on those directories, you can complete the process as described above: look for your church, claim your name, and revise. Google considers these listings to be relevant but not quite as important. Search and find the most relevant directories for your church online from the millions of directories available. A listing might also be included on your denomination's website or in your association.

Churches need to ask for reviews from their congregation for higher ranking on Google Local Pack. It is important enough that they should do it during Sunday morning services, because this creates social proof that there are many people at the church who vary in personality type and age group, just like any other business would want. I also recommend following up on a negative review as soon as possible so you can engage with your prospective members effectively before anything escalates further.

There is even more you can do to help your church rank higher in Google's SERP, but we will discuss that later in the chapter on websites. Google's Local Pack plays an important role in your future visitors' decision on what church to visit. Reviewing other church listings, auditing your listing, claiming your listing, revising your NAP data, adding photos, signing up for other directories, and asking for more reviews will help your church rise in the rankings.

Building a Content Strategy

There are numerous ways to effectively communicate within and about your church. Without a doubt, it should be done through social media. Social media and the Internet have changed how we communicate. The good news is, church leaders do not have to be technological specialists to put effective content strategies into practice.

Likes and views do not miraculously turn into church growth. Churches must leverage social media and their websites to reach new people for the gospel. They must be able to overcome common pitfalls, challenges, and dead ends that are often faced when creating a content strategy. There is tremendous value in understanding why churches are online and how they use their online presence to grow.

If you think about it, our friend Paul from the Bible was a content strategist himself. He was always writing letters and using the latest innovations of his day to spread the hope of the gospel in new and exciting ways. Now it is our turn to take up that mantle and follow in his footsteps of carrying the gospel to the ends of the earth and the Internet.

What Is a Content Strategy?

A content strategy simply defined is having a plan for your content. The church is actually one of the world's largest media and publishing houses ever created. Every week, pastors around the world publish and create new content about the Bible, but what if it did not have to stop on Sunday? Sunday mornings have been what the church has revolved around for centuries, but church is not just a service on a Sunday morning. The church is a people group who are alive and breathing, and we exist outside the constructs of one, two, or three hours on a Sunday. We need to create a content strategy that empowers and educates our church members to live out out our mission every day.

Have you ever heard of omnichannel? *Omnichannel* is a retail marketing term for being in more places than just one. Originally, we just had retail stores, but then along came catalogs, television, and then the Internet. Every company that wanted to stay in business needed to take an omnichannel approach to the way they were doing business. In that same way, so does the church. Jesus told us to go to the ends of the earth, and we can get to the ends of the earth via the Internet if we intentionally create plans and content to do that.

The first question, which we've already discussed, is, who is your target audience? Who will be watching, reading, and consuming the church's content as it is produced? What age are they? What kind of content do they enjoy? Just as you and your children might prefer different types of media, such as TV or reading a book, so do our target audiences.

The second question to answer is, what problems will you be solving with your content? Many churches produce content every week without answering any of the questions their members actually have. Can we use the content that is already being produced (like the weekly sermon) to answer those questions? Should we create additional content on our website, for YouTube, or for a podcast to help answer those questions? Content should educate and empower our audiences to help them in their discipleship process.

The third question should be taken from your mission and vision: What makes your church unique? There are several churches in your area, but what kind of content can you create that no other church can? Maybe there is a podcaster in your church who can create a podcast that your church can include on its website. Maybe you have an excellent organist who could create beautiful renditions of hymns with a short gospel message in them that you upload to YouTube. Maybe your pastor shares timely and relevant topical messages every week in a devotional format via email. Could the pastor also do these as a Facebook Live video that then gets uploaded to YouTube and also sent out via email? Creating content unique to your church will help set your church apart.

The fourth question is, what kind of content will you create? Should your church write a blog? Start a YouTube Channel? Use Facebook and Instagram? There are many different types of content: blogging, infographics, case studies, e-books, checklists, videos, memes, photo galleries, event roundups, podcasts, online and offline magazines, social media, reviews, mind maps, news releases, inspirational messages, quotes, fliers, wikis—the list goes on and on. Identify the topics your church can take a position on, and then set aside a budget to create that content. For your website, it is essential to write content based on felt needs in your community. When people search for needs like "parenting help," "need help paying bills," or "prayer," your church should be the website or YouTube video that answers their needs. Content strategy can help us find people with needs in our community. If your church doesn't have a budget for creating content, ask for volunteers. This is not necessarily something a church has to pay for. Often your best source of content is your current church members.

The fifth question is, on what channel will you publish? We discuss channel evaluation in chapter 4, but there are more than just social media channels to choose from. Choosing the right medium for your message is often just as important, if not more so, as crafting the right message.

Creating a content strategy does not have to be difficult. Using a spreadsheet or a calendar can be very useful. Write down the church calendar, including Easter and Christmas, and make a note of all other major events. Use those dates to count back six to eight weeks to create a content strategy or promotional calendar for each event. Creating a content strategy can be as easy as creating a daily or monthly schedule. For example, a daily schedule might look like this:

- *Monday—social media*: Recap the Sunday sermon; final deadline to receive weekly bulletin content
- *Tuesday—social media*: Share a promotional event reminder; send a reminder text about event
- *Wednesday—social media*: Remind students and parents about Wednesday night activities; send weekly email
- *Thursday—social media*: Throwback Thursday—share a vintage photo and celebrate the church's history; print and fold bulletins; walk through church cleaning up old messaging and putting out new messaging where appropriate
- *Friday—social media:* Looking forward to Sunday, what is coming up this weekend?
- *Saturday—social media*: Invite Saturday—share a way to invite a friend to church
- *Sunday—social media*: Share the livestream and photos taken in the moment

Creating a monthly schedule can be accomplished just as easily:

- *Week 1*: Focus on the new sermon series
- *Week 2*: Focus on a missions event
- *Week 3*: Focus on student ministry
- *Week 4*: Focus on children's ministry

It may seem daunting to create a content strategy at first, but it is straightforward once you begin planning. Both content and promotion are simple when you use a calendar and plan ahead. To start, it is essential to collect information about key dates from all the ministry leaders during the strategy-development stage. Once you are implementing the strategy via the calendar, it will be more difficult to change the plan but not impossible.

Media Release Forms

While we are on the topic of content, we should address some legalities. The problem with creating content is that you often will need pictures and videos to include in that content. But you shouldn't take pictures or videos of anyone, especially children, without a media release. A media consent release, or media release, is a legally binding document that grants the rights to produce, reproduce, edit, and publish videos of an individual. You should use a media release form for planned events if and when possible. You could also post a sign at the event that pictures and video will be taken. Depending on your local laws, the church visitor may sign the form before or immediately after participating in an event. I am not offering legal advice since I am not an attorney, but it is important to reach out to a local attorney to create media release forms. You can find an example of a release on the Church Communications website at https://churchcommunications .com/media-release-forms/.

Email Marketing

Your ministry can benefit significantly from email marketing when it is executed correctly. Churches are notorious for sending out "bad email," such as newsletters that have the same subject line every week like "First Baptist Church Newsletter" or "Week of November 6." However, when emails are done right, they can not only educate your congregation on your church and its events but excite them enough to share them with their friends and family. So, how can we do email well?

With new, flashy forms of communication, email marketing is something that seems old as time itself, but it is actually still extremely relevant and useful today. Email can be checked anywhere at any time, making it the ultimate form of communication. OptinMonster, a leading communicative technology company that has helped over one million businesses gain subscribers (retain email addresses), reports that 99 percent of email users check their email at least once a day; it is not just used to send virtual birthday party invites anymore. In fact, 61 percent of consumers prefer to be contacted by email from businesses, with 50 percent of emails being read on mobile devices.[2]

Email marketing is one of the most practical platforms for communication. It is inexpensive and effective, which makes it a perfect form of communication for nonprofit organizations, churches, or even the largest businesses in the world. It is successfully measurable and controlled, and it allows the organization to segment its audiences. For example, if you want to create an announcement about a women's night out, you can send it to only women in your organization.

Before writing out email marketing material, you need to have a list of contacts to send it to. Make sure your teams are continually asking for email addresses. You cannot communicate with a congregation to which you do not have virtual access. Build up that contact list by gaining emails through event sign-ups, next-steps cards, Facebook Events, and so on. Remember, users do have to agree to their email address being used, so make sure that your church is complying with the Federal Trade Commission and CAN-SPAM Act. Get your list, comply with regulations, and use the following sections to write compelling emails.

First, create an email schedule, and stick to it. Be consistent, but be consistent with relevant and worthwhile information. Be clear and concise. If readers wanted to read a book, they would not be in their inbox. According to OptinMonster, the top three reasons people unsubscribe from email lists are that they receive too many emails, the information is no longer relevant, or the consumer does not remember

---

[2] Allison Hott, "40+ Email Marketing Statistics You Need to Know for 2021," OptinMonster, January 6, 2021, https://optinmonster.com/email-marketing-statistics.

signing up.[3] Send your email subscribers content they want, not aimless, untargeted messages. Have a mission and use words that hold value; be succinct and bring messages with merit, not junk mail, to their inbox. Content can include milestones for the church, newsletters, events happening that month, announcements, and more. Make sure to include links to information you are discussing, when possible. Talking about signing kids up for VBS? Embed the link to sign-ups in the words "Sign up now!" that came with the announcement. Do not make consumers dig for the bare minimum information. They most likely will not put in the effort to find the extra information, and you will miss out on an easy sign-up.

Subject lines must be exciting. Have you ever seen a boring subject line from a store that just says, "30 percent off until Sunday" and sent it straight to the trash without opening it? Me too. But if I see an intriguing subject line like "The outfit that will turn heads is 30 percent off now through Sunday!" you can bet your last dollar I'll open that email, which will most likely lead me to their landing page. The same concept applies to emails you send to the congregation. "The Sunday News for Christ Church of Oakland." That sounds pretty boring. "What Did Jesus Say about Broken Relationships?" "Five Tips to Get Your Kids Psyched about VBS." That is much more intriguing! Get creative; you only have so much time to grab readers' attention, so use it wisely. You can even go a step further and personalize the subject line. According to MarketingDive.com, "Personalizing email subject lines can increase open rates by 50% and lead to 58% higher click-to-open rates."[4]

If your church does not already have a provider for email marketing, many services are available, including AWeber (free for 500 contacts), MailChimp (free for under 2,000 contacts), Vertical Response (free for under 4,000 contacts), Constant Contact, ConvertKit, Active Campaign, SendinBlue, and Infusionsoft.[5] These are great options for sending large quantities of email marketing. They allow for all email addresses to remain private so you are not sharing everyone's email

---

[3] Jacinda Santora, "Is Email Marketing Dead? Statistics Say: Not a Chance," OptinMonster, August 14, 2020, https://optinmonster.com/is-email-marketing-dead-heres-what-the-statistics-show.

[4] David Kirkpatrick, "Study: Personalized Email Subject Lines Increase Open Rates by 50%," Marketing Dive, September 12, 2017, https://www.marketingdive.com/news/study-personalized-email-subject-lines-increase-open-rates-by-50/504714.

[5] The easiest and most cost affordable for the majority of churches is MailChimp.com.

with the congregation as well. These services help comply with privacy laws and also give you helpful feedback about recipients, with metrics such as what percent opened the email, what percent clicked into the links provided, if your email just sits in a spam folder, and more.

Digital marketing includes social media, email marketing, website content, and so much more. We will explore these topics further in future chapters.

Chapter 4

Social Media

What Is Social Media?

Social media consists of various platforms that perform different ways of networking and promotion, and it is also a means of electronic communication and connection. Social media includes both earned and paid media. It is earned because a marketer has to work to gain a following, and it is paid because a marketer can also pay to gain a following.

A social media marketing campaign for a church involves promoting the church and its content via social media channels for the purpose of increasing brand awareness, driving traffic, and getting more people to hear about Jesus. Social media marketing has many channels, including Facebook, YouTube, Twitter, LinkedIn, Instagram, Snapchat, Pinterest, and TikTok. Social media is the most popular form of communication today. Having a strong social media presence has become a necessity for churches and Christians.

Data from Statista.com showed that in 2020 an estimated 3.81 billion people around the globe used social media.[1] There is no escaping social media. Many people use social media to experience church, find a date, follow the news, or merely because they are bored. People spend a lot of time on social media; I'm sure if you look at your time spent on social media this past week, you might be embarrassed by it. But here's the key: if people change how they communicate and live, the church will have to as well. The last thirty years have completely revolutionized how we communicate as a culture—emojis, texting, websites, and social media.

Why You Should Use Social Media for Your Church

According to Pew Research, "Roughly seven-in-ten Americans say they ever use any kind of social media site—a share that has remained relatively stable over the past five years." That same research reported the three most popular platforms were YouTube (81 percent), Facebook (69 percent), and Instagram (40 percent).[2]

Social media is where people are, so it is where the church should also be. A church's social media is the front line for reaching people today. Churches and businesses often see social media like a billboard, but social media is different from a static billboard—it is interactive! You cannot talk to a billboard, but you can talk to and reach millions of people through social media.

The apostle Paul sent letters using the most advanced technology of his day (the Roman roads) and we too must use our technology (social media) to reach people far from Christ. Are you using YouTube, Facebook, Instagram, and other social media platforms to share the gospel? If so, are you using it strategically? I do not mean just uploading your sermons every week, but intentionally creating pieces of content to answer gospel-centered questions.

[1] Simon O'Dea, "Forecast Number of Mobile Users Worldwide 2020–2025," Statista, July 12, 2021, https://www.statista.com/statistics/218984/number-of-global-mobile-users-since-2010.

[2] Brooke Auxier and Monica Anderson, "Social Media Use in 2021," Pew Research Center, April 7, 2021, https://www.pewresearch.org/internet/2021/04/07//social-media-use-in-2021/.

Compelling Data to Conclude and Push Us Onward

During the second week of the COVID-19 pandemic, online searches including the word *prayer* surged to an all-time high—100 percent interest. Here's a screenshot of that chart as of August 2020.[3]

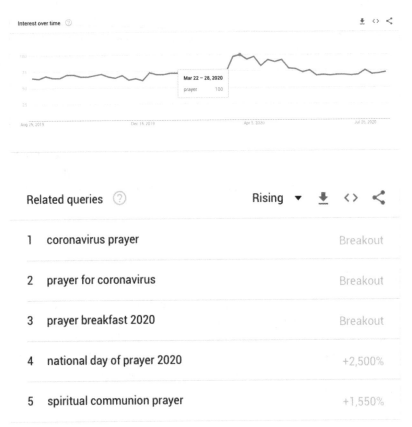

It was incredible. A revival was happening, but we did not have the content online to support it. Jesus told his disciples, "The harvest is abundant, but the workers are few" (Matt 9:37). That was true about churches' social media usage when the pandemic began. Not many churches were using social media to its full extent before the pandemic: many churches were not livestreaming, and many were not

---

[3] "Google Trends," Google Trends, August 19, 2020, https://trends.google.com/trends /explore?q=prayer&geo=US.

intentionally making plans to reach their community using social media as a platform. People went online in search of hope and answers. Did they find them on your church website, on your social media, or on YouTube?

We will go deeper into how we can use social media more effectively, but for now, I want you to pray about this. The harvest online is plentiful, but the majority of our churches weren't prepared to reach the masses online when they needed it. Let's never let that happen again.

Channel Evaluation

Not all channels are the same. It can be overwhelming to decide if your congregation should establish an online presence using Facebook, Instagram, WhatsApp, LinkedIn, Snapchat, or Pinterest. Churches do not need to be on every channel. Many churches feel compelled to be on every channel, but if they are on every channel, they will likely not do any of them well. Strategy for each channel is different, as we will discuss in this chapter.

What Are the Social Channels Available?

Many social channels exist, and by the time this book comes out, many more channels probably will be available. There are social media apps you may never have known existed, many of which are popular in Eastern countries, such as WhatsApp, WeChat, and QQ. WhatsApp has been gaining traction in the United States since it was bought by Facebook in February 2014.[4]

How Should Your Church Decide What Social Channels to Use?

What are your church's goals? What are your social media strategy objectives, and how are they tied to the church's goals? It is essential for churches to tie their social media channels to their overall goals. If you can't articulate why or how a certain channel would help your church achieve its goals, you probably should not use it.

---

[4] Josh Constine, "A Year Later, $19 Billion for WhatsApp Doesn't Sound So Crazy," TechCrunch, February 20, 2015, https://techcrunch.com/2015/02/19/crazy-like-a-facebook-fox.

What Social Channels Is Your Target Audience Using?

Once you identify where your audience is interacting online, you need to coordinate your goals with your social channel selection. For instance, if your church is primarily older women, creating a TikTok account would be a waste of time. Using Pinterest might be ineffective if your church is primarily composed of men.

To quote the Little Mermaid, "I want to be where the people are." You have to determine where your people are using social media. What channels are they using? This is easily done in a congregational survey by asking what social channels your members are using. Try limiting it to a list of the top five such as Facebook, Instagram, YouTube, Twitter, and TikTok.

What Social Channels Are Other Churches Using?

Conduct a social media evaluation of other churches by creating a spreadsheet to compare what other churches in your area and denomination are using.

	FACEBOOK	INSTAGRAM	TWITTER	TIKTOK	YOUTUBE
FIRST BAPTIST	1,685	2,809	128	345	54
SARALAND BAPTIST	2,800	4,500	328	0	256
SARALAND UNITED METHODIST	3,450	3,200	0	0	0

After you have done a little social media detective work, you should quickly see what social media channels are working for churches in your area and denomination. This should make it fairly easy to decide what channels to use. I recommend gathering information from at least ten churches in your area and at least five churches in your denomination of similar size.

What Kind of Content Does the Church Want to Create? What Is Already Working for the Church?

Look at the first question: what kind of content does the church want to create? The church can create images for Instagram, Facebook, or Pinterest. It can create shorter content for Twitter or Facebook. It can create videos for YouTube, TikTok, Facebook, or Instagram. It can create blogs for Medium.com. The platform medium determines how well the message is accepted and understood. Choose the right type of medium for the church's message and unique style of communication.

Consider YouTube, TikTok, Facebook, and Instagram if the church wants to create and share video content. The video length will determine where the church should post the content. If the video is shorter and targeted more toward a younger audience, Instagram, Snapchat, or TikTok might be a better platform, but if it is longer and more universal, consider Facebook or YouTube. YouTube is the second-largest search engine, with more than three billion searches per month.[5]

If you're looking for ways to share your church content on social media, consider the following. Facebook is a great option if you want to post heavy content like events or devotionals. Twitter works well with lighter topics such as quotes and Scripture verses that are short in length. Instagram and Pinterest work best when sharing images of anything from Bible passages to pictures of food at church events— although they each prefer different types of content! Experiment with what type of image-based content performs best on your church's platforms by trying things out over time; it may be one platform in particular but could also depend on the topic being shared. You might find some interesting results after experimenting with various forms of imagery across multiple channels.

How Many Channels Can You Manage?

It is unlikely that a single social channel will suffice for your church, but figuring out a mix of channels and striking a balance can be difficult. Too many social media channels will dilute your message and confuse your audience, but with too few you risk losing brand awareness and reach.

In the Church Communications Facebook Group, we did a quick poll to determine how many social channels churches were using. We

---

[5] "YouTube: The 2nd Largest Search Engine (Infographic)," Mushroom Networks, accessed March 22, 2021, https://www.mushroomnetworks.com/infographics /youtube---the-2nd-largest-search-engine-infographic.

found out that three social channels—Facebook, Instagram, and You-Tube—are primarily used by churches.[6]

There are many social media tools to help make posting to multiple channels more straightforward—for example, Buffer, Hootsuite, Agora Pulse, Sprout Social, and Later. These allow you to schedule posts in advance and cross post content across social channels. Cross posting can be dangerous because content that works on Instagram does not always work on Facebook and vice versa. Each platform has its own way of working, and sometimes it is better if you tailor the content to the forum. Most social media management platforms allow you to upload photos, video, and so on, which is essential to consider because content with relevant images gets 94 percent more views than content with no pictures.[7]

Juggling different social media channels can be overwhelming. To succeed, you need to create a unique experience across all platforms rather than simply posting the same Bible verse graphic on every platform with no caption. This is why you need a strategy.

Social Metrics

In social media advertising, companies use statistics, demographics, and other data to cultivate consumer-seller relationships. However, for churches, social media should function differently. When a church engages in social media platforms, it is a mistake to measure its engagement by focusing on the number of people in your congregation or the number of views on your sermon livestream. Not only is this approach very results oriented, but it also removes the relationship element from the equation. People become numbers, and the welfare of those faces behind the screen gets lost in the rising tally. Relegating people to a colored graph or seat count will not only foster a feeling of detachment in church leaders, but also in the people you have recruited to your church.

When your church enters into social media and social media advertising, it is important to remember what your goal is: to create

---

6 "Church Communications Facebook Group," Facebook, accessed March 22, 2021, https://www.facebook.com/groups/churchcomm/permalink/1499869570196636.

7 Jesse Mawhinney, "50 Visual Content Marketing Statistics You Should Know in 2021," *HubSpot* (blog), February 16, 2021, https://blog.hubspot.com/marketing/visual-content-marketing-strategy.

long-lasting relationships. SocialChurch.com equated concentrating on a head count to proposing on the first date. By rushing the development of the relationship with your potential new member, you risk losing them just as quickly as you drew them in. Cultivating that relationship is where measuring your church's social media engagement becomes helpful.[8]

Measuring your engagement with your posts, tweets, and website can indicate where and how your followers and potential churchgoers feel most connected. To expand on the previous metaphor of dating, think of it like virtually dating your leads. With any and all dates, they are going to have likes and dislikes. One date may love flowers; another might be allergic and prefer chocolates. By measuring your social media engagement, you have the ability to figure out what is and is not working in your relationships.

Once you start paying attention—once you start documenting and tracking these trends—what is nourishing your relationship with your followers and what is harming it will become much clearer.

What Metrics to Measure

Audience Size

The number of followers on social media platforms is one metric that churches are actually good at measuring. Of course, these numbers are good to look at because they will give you a rough estimate of who your current audience is. However, the audience size does not tell the whole story.

By relying solely on the number of followers your church has or the number of people who show up for service, you ignore those leads who may not be quite there yet. They are interested in your church, but they are not ready to wear the diamond ring yet. So, yes, this will give you a solid indication of who is in the body of your church, but it will not show you the totality of your engagement.

Post Reach

With post reach, you come much closer to gauging the true size of your audience. These analytics will tell you how many impressions

---

[8] "Is Social Media Worth It? Measuring Social Media ROI for Churches," Social Church, May 8, 2019, https://socialchurch.com/is-social-media-worth-it-measuring-social-media-roi-for -churches.

you got on a post and how many people saw it. Because of how social media platforms are structured, not everyone will see your post. It is a bit paradoxical. The more people engage with your post, the more other people will see your post; however, for people to see your post, other people first have to interact with it.

Regardless, with post reach, your audience size is much more accurately measured. You might have 5,000 followers, but if you only have 1,000 impressions on your posts, that is closer to your true audience size.

Engagement

This is what you are after. If there were a formula for the perfect post with the perfect caption, it would be a post that every single person would like, share, and comment on. Engaging means you have taken your relationship one step closer to commitment. No longer are followers satisfied with being anonymous bystanders; your content is so compelling that they have to show their friends or show their appreciation by liking or commenting on it.

Where post reach can show you who is seeing your content, engagement lets you know who is investing in your content. This is important because it demonstrates what kinds of posts are working for your church. By studying the posts that are provoking the most engagement, you can replicate that formula in the future and hopefully attract more like-minded folks to your page and eventually to your church.

Website Traffic

The final metric you should monitor is traffic to your website. When you post on social media platforms, it is beneficial to direct followers and leads to your website. Sharing blog posts from your website on your Facebook page or having a link in your Instagram bio is a good way to offer more content while increasing your reach and engagement with the eventual goal of conversion.

Establish a Plan

Measuring these metrics and keeping track of all the analytics can seem daunting. However, if your church establishes a method of tracking, organizing, and processing the data, measuring the metrics will not only help you grow your church, it will also help you deepen relationships within your community.[9]

Conversions

Differentiating between conversion and engagement can be confusing. The key difference between conversion and engagement is action versus superficial action. Conversion means that your lead, your new follower, is ready to take it a step beyond commenting, sharing, and liking, which are actions requiring little to no commitment. For churches, conversion can look like signing up for community service projects, volunteering to work in the nursery once a month, or participating in a small group.

Whatever the activity, conversion requires real commitment and a real-time investment. The point of measuring your metrics is to determine whether a person is truly connected—hook, line, and sinker. Of course, like any relationship, that does not mean you neglect the cultivation and maintenance of this relationship. However, you know this person is much less likely to lose interest than someone who is engaging with your posts but not your church community as a whole.

Remember, with this measuring technique, it is necessary to not only look at and record your digital measurements but also document who is showing up for your small groups, volunteer efforts, and so on. While this might feel a little like playing Big Brother, it will ultimately give you a better picture of what is and is not working for your church outreach programs.

Paid Social

Perhaps you've heard this popular expression: "The world is overrun with technology." Expressions like this are often filed away as hyperbolic. According to a study conducted by Statista, "In 2019, there were 2.82 billion social media users worldwide, 6.8 billion mobile phone users, and the high usage of Web 2.0 technologies."[10] These statistics suggest the expression is not an exaggeration but rather a commentary on the growing usage of and dependence on technological devices.

---

[9] Robert Cairnes, "Measuring Your Church's Success on Social Media," *Orange Leaders* (blog), March 23, 2017, https://orangeblogs.org/orangeleaders/2017/03/23/measuring-your -churchs-success-on-social-media.

[10] Statista Research Department, "U.S. Snapchat Usage by Age 2020," Statista, January 28, 2021, https://www.statista.com/statistics/814300/snapchat-users-in-the-united-states-by-age.

According to Webfx.com, advertisements can be paid for on seven different standards:[11]

1. Cost-per-click (CPC): You pay every time someone clicks on your ad.
2. Cost-per-thousand-impressions (CPM): You pay every time 1,000 people see your ad.
3. Cost-per-like (CPL): You pay every time someone likes your post.
4. Cost-per-action (CPA): You pay every time someone completes your desired action, like a purchase.
5. Cost-per-engagement (CPE): You pay every time someone interacts with your ad.
6. Cost-per-follower (CPF): You pay every time someone uses your advertisement to follow your business.
7. Cost-per-download (CPD): You pay when someone downloads something, like an app.

Large companies and organizations often select CPM, so their advertisements are seen the most and are therefore at the forefront of the customers' minds. However, for churches or smaller companies, selecting the CPC option can be a much more cost-effective method.[12]

How It Works

Social media platforms such as Instagram and Facebook allow the user to customize their ads and who sees those ads. This means it is that much easier to target the demographic you are hoping to draw to your church. Looking to fill your congregation with millennial women who shop at Old Navy and Ulta and have a penchant for Hershey's chocolate? You can do that.

However, before you determine whom you want to target with your campaign, you should choose which ad or series of ads you want to feature. What is the goal of this campaign? Whom are you trying to draw in? What series, small group, or other church feature are you highlighting?

---

[11] "How Much Does Social Media Advertising Cost in 2021?," WebFX, accessed September 23, 2021, https://www.webfx.com/how-much-does-social-media-advertising-cost.html.
[12] "How Much Does Social Media Advertising Cost in 2021?"

Once you have nailed down the goal of the campaign and the content of the ad(s), the next step is to decide on the target demographic; a subset of a demographic is going to be most receptive to your ad.

Choosing the right target audience is going to be key to the success of your advertisement. Targeting single women out of New Jersey with an ad that features your Alabama church's series on biblical marriages probably is not the best plan. However, young women in their early twenties who live in New Jersey and have been searching for wedding dresses, rings, and florists could yield more clicks, subscriptions, and engagements.

The Investment

Paid advertising on social media is cost effective for reaching large audiences in just one campaign. It can be less expensive than traditional marketing methods, and you don't even need to have an audience before getting started! It does not take a lot of money to reach a lot of people; it just takes planning and ingenuity.

Fishers of Men

According to a recent statistic, "More than 70 percent of nonprofit communicators consider social media one of their most important communication channels."[13] The easiest way to become a well-known brand is by communicating on social media, right now. As a church, it is our job to meet people where they are, and having a social media presence that stands out is one of the most effective ways to do that.

Additionally, the Pew Research Center found that "88 percent of 18- to 29-year-olds in the U.S. use some form of social media."[14] This study tells churches that the younger generations who are starting new families or will be starting new families rely heavily on technology. This is important for churches to acknowledge, because the future of the body of Christ will depend heavily on building a foundation of

---

[13] Andrew Conrad, "10 Powerful Church Statistics on Social Media Use," *Church Management* (blog), Capterra, March 13, 2018, https://blog.capterra.com/church-statistics-social-media.

[14] Aaron Smith and Monica Anderson, "Social Media Use in 2018," Pew Research Center, March 1, 2018, https://www.pewresearch.org/internet/wp-content/uploads/sites/9/2018/02/PI_2018.03.01_Social-Media_FINAL.pdf.

faith in the new generations of churchgoers. But to build that foundation, you first must get people to church.

Jesus called his disciples to be fishers of men, and the way we fish looks different now. Although this process of paid advertising may seem daunting at first, consider the benefits: by using the enhanced targeting system to increase your accuracy, your church will be much more capable of reeling in new followers.

Facebook

Should churches use Facebook?When I posed this question to my Facebook Group, Church Communications, I immediately got the reply, "That kind of feels like the wrong question. What is it you are trying to achieve, and what's the best way for that to happen?" And yes, it is important to know what we are trying to achieve and how we can make it happen, but it is also important to know why we are on this platform to begin with. I think my preferred answer from that thread was from my friend Nick Roe: "Jesus said 'go.'"[15]

People are on Facebook. According to Facebook, over three billion people use Facebook.[16] Church leaders should invest in social media. With over three billion people on Facebook, it's a great way for your church to reach out and connect with others around the world.

You probably know what Facebook is, but did you know that Facebook has different verticals or products?[17] Facebook's main product—what you are probably the most familiar with—is the Timeline. It is what you see immediately when you log in (it is what you scroll through endlessly when you are bored), but there is so much more to Facebook than just the Timeline. Here are some of the many other products on Facebook:

* Personal Profile
* Pages
* Groups
* Marketplace

---

[15] "Church Communications Facebook Group," Facebook, accessed March 22, 2021, https://www.facebook.com/groups/churchcomm/permalink/1499869570196636.

[16] "Company Info," Facebook, February 10, 2021, https://about.fb.com/company-info.

[17] Facebook has a whole department working around the clock to help faith-based organizations. Facebook wants to help you share the gospel. You can learn more and access those resources at https://www.facebook.com/community/faith.

- Dating
- Messenger
- WhatsApp
- Instagram

There are three main Facebook products that we should focus on as a church: the Personal Profile, your church's Page, Ads, and Groups. That does not mean the other platforms are useless; ministry can definitely take place via Messenger or even Marketplace, but for our purposes, we are going to focus on the primary means.[18]

Before we go over the primary Facebook products to use for your church, it should be stated that Facebook offers tons of free resources to learn how to use their products on Facebook Blueprint. Facebook Blueprint offers free courses and also paid certifications in different products. You can access these resources by going to https://www.facebook.com/business/learn.

Personal Profile

The Personal Profile is the most ubiquitous product that Facebook is known for. You set up your Personal Profile when you open a Facebook account. It consists of a personal feed, your cover image, and your profile image, as well as photos, videos, and information.

Churches should not use Personal Profile; your church should use a Page. Personal Profiles are limited to 5,000 friends, and even if you are sure that your church will never reach that limit, it still goes against the terms of use. Facebook Personal Profiles were meant to be just that—"personal" and meant for "persons" (people), not businesses or organizations.

That does not mean the church cannot use Personal Profiles; it just means we need to get creative in how we use them. On Facebook, some content is favored over others by the engine's algorithm. It is in our best interest to work with that algorithm and not against it. In terms of algorithms, from my own personal experience, Facebook

---

[18] If you are doing international ministry, it would make sense to invest in and learn WhatsApp, a Facebook product. WhatsApp is a messaging service similar to Messenger that has gained traction with the international community as a means of sending free messages through a WiFi or cell data connection.

prefers Personal Profile content posted in the timeline best, followed by Group content, followed by Page and Ad content.

Since we already established that a church should have a Page and not a Profile, how can Profiles be used to work with the algorithm to promote a church's content for free? You need to create an intentional strategy to empower church members to share content and good news.

Imagine that Easter is coming up. You can ask members to change their Profile pictures to an image about the Easter service. Facebook highly values Profile image changes since they are not usually very frequent, so it will show this to all of a person's friends. If your church has 100 members, and each of them changes their Profile picture, and each of those members have 100 friends (assuming no overlap), that means you could potentially reach 10,000 people. In reality, people usually have a lot more friends than that on Facebook.

Another strategy to use for Easter is to create a Facebook Event on the church's Page and then ask the congregation to click "interested" or "going" all at the same time during the morning worship service. This will show the Event to all of their friends and people in the surrounding area. If lots of people hit that they are interested at the same time, Facebook will think this is a hot Event and start showing it to others in the area.

Another strategy for using the Personal Profile is to share the church's livestream and Page content. Personal Profiles can create "watch parties" and invite other people to watch with them in their own special feed with their own chat room. Remind church members that sharing, liking, and commenting on the church's content helps spread the gospel.

Finally, the best strategy to use on Facebook to spread the gospel is this: ask, "What can I be praying for you?" Encouraging your members to reach out to their friends and post on their own Personal Profiles about prayer is the best and simplest strategy for reaching people for the gospel. People want to be prayed for, but often they are too shy or afraid to ask. Encourage members to give people the opportunity to be prayed for and prayed with. I encourage people to do this weekly and then to follow up on those prayer requests.

Pages

Facebook Pages are often seen as the front door of a church. Long gone are the days of fancy marquee signs; today the best investment a church can make is in a Facebook Page strategy. Facebook Pages are like Personal Profiles with superpowers like scheduling in Creator Tools, livestreaming using Facebook Live, and creating a following that can reach hundreds or thousands or even millions.

Having a Facebook Page for your church offers many benefits. It could be the first thing a potential guest sees about a church. It could also be where you livestream Sunday services as well as post any church announcements. So many people use Facebook, which is why it is incredibly important for churches to have a strong presence there.

In 2018, it was reported that almost 84 percent of churches have a Facebook Page.[19] Facebook Pages are a great tool and resource, and they are also necessary for sharing the gospel. Many churches use Facebook Live for streaming their worship services, and they use their Pages as the medium to display that livestream.

A Page is where the church should share stories of life change, what God is doing, and how he is moving in your congregation. It is not a great announcement platform for sharing important information with your congregation. Facebook Pages are primarily for outreach. A church's Facebook Page helps tell the story of what Christ is doing in that church, but it is not the best for internal communication. Facebook Groups, email, and text messaging are better at internal communication.

Facebook Pages have many feature sets:

- Check-ins
- Reviews
- Events
- Facebook Live
- Status updates

Check-ins are what happens when a user selects that they are at your church in a status update. The check-in feature notifies others that members of your church are attending services, and that results in free advertisement and brand awareness for the church. Unfortunately, many times users are not actually at your church, and the Facebook Page administrator cannot remove these check-ins.

---

[19] Bob Smietana, "Most Churches Offer WiFi but Skip Twitter," Lifeway Research, January 9, 2018, https://lifewayresearch.com/2018/01/09/most-churches-offer-free-wi-fi-but-skip-twitter.

Many churches create multiple Facebook Pages for each ministry. I recommend against doing that. You will lose your organic reach, and your audience will be split among multiple pages. I recommend creating one main Facebook Page for your church and then creating several Facebook Groups for communicating internally with your ministries. You can then connect these Groups to your Page.[20]

Groups

If Facebook Pages are the front door for your church, then Facebook Groups are the living room. Facebook Groups are an excellent tool for internal communication with your congregation. They are also an excellent tool for outreach. We will go over both of these strategies.

As stated in the previous section on Facebook Pages, your church should have one Page with many Groups. Give these Groups clear and concise names. We learned in the "Brand Extensions" section of the branding chapter that the Internet and people in general desire to have clear names, not cute names.

First, think through the Facebook Groups you would like to create. Next, decide on an additional administrator for each Group. Groups require a lot of work, and you will need other administrators to take on some of this. Then, discuss your plan with that ministry and support person. For example, it would make sense to create a Children's Ministry Group for your children's ministry and for the administrator to be your children's minister.

After you have informed and discussed the benefits of having a Group with your new administrator, create the Group, and link it to your Page. You can link the Group to your Page inside either the Group or Page settings. Next, you will need to write an informative description and some rules for your Group. Consider writing a description that includes your church's name, the administrator's contact information, and what the Group is for.

Facebook creates generic rules to follow in a Group. Rules are important when moderating an online discussion. Rules will naturally come about in your Group as you start shaping the culture and online environment you want the Group to take on. You can change the generic rules and add to them.

---

[20] For more information on how to set up a Facebook Page, see appendix E.

Do not only think about what people cannot do in your Group when creating rules, but consider what they can do. Often, we forget that real people are behind the screen, so it is important to remember that. Rules may seem mundane, but think of them more like boundaries and expectations. You are not only telling people what they cannot do but what they can do.

When setting up a Group, there are two important configurations: setting your Group as public or private, then setting your Group as visible or hidden. A public Group means that everyone can access all the posts and all the members of that Group can also share posts in that Group to their own Profiles or Pages. A public Group has much in common with a Facebook Page except that it does not have reviews or check-ins. A private Group, on the other hand, is more exclusive. No one can see the content inside the Group before joining, but outsiders can see the members in that Group before joining it. The visible or hidden settings are all about searchability, or how someone can find your Group. If you want your Group to be listed on your church's Page and you want someone to be able to find your Group by searching Facebook, it should be a visible Group. If you do not want anyone to be able to find the Group, that should be a hidden Group. Most Groups you create should be private and visible, but sometimes you might need a hidden Group. For example, if you have a Group of missionaries, a hidden closed Group might be more appropriate. For church ministry purposes, I recommend creating a private visible Group. For outreach purposes, a public visible Group might be better.

Using Facebook Groups for Your Congregation and Ministries
Facebook Pages can run advertisements, while Groups cannot. Groups were created for bringing people together. If you have a multi-campus church, I still recommend creating both a Page and a Group for the campus because Pages can have reviews and check-ins, while Groups cannot.

Groups also have a lot of great features like social learning tools. You can create a course right inside your Facebook Group, and your members can go through that course. You can see who has and has not completed each course you create in the Group. You can use this to create an online Bible study for your Sunday School class or maybe a focused study on a certain subject. You can also go live in a Facebook Group, which is great if you are a Bible study leader. You can then organize those live videos into course modules in your Group so that members can view them later.

For example, your church might have a choir. You can create a Group to share sheet music, wardrobe changes, and so on. The church social media manager can then use this Group to share more information from your church's Page. For instance, create an Event on your Page, and share that Event with the Group. It will then appear in the Group's Events. Ask everyone to click that they are going to the Event. I did this with Easter at a church where I worked and reached several thousand people without paying any money in ads. Not only are Facebook Groups good for creating community, but they are also great at sharing information and engaging your community.

If you create a Facebook Group for your ministry, you will want to ensure it stays active and engaged. In order to do that, you will need to create content on a regular basis. You can create weekly topics for people to engage with. Continuing with the choir example, a weekly post might be, "What was your favorite song from this past week?" or "What song would you like us to sing next week?" If you have a preschool parents' group, a weekly topic might be, "What crazy thing did your child do this week? Share a photo in the comments." Creating weekly topic ideas helps facilitate and create engagement easily. Many tools can be used to post weekly content. Content that never goes out of style or out of date and that can be used again and again is called "evergreen content." Try finding a social media scheduler that schedules evergreen content, such as SocialBee, MeetEdgar, or RecurPost.

Using Facebook Groups to Reach Your Community
We have already established that there are billions of people using social media. Facebook Groups can be used to reach many people who are not connected to us in our community.

In order to do this, you should think about something you, your church, or even your small group is passionate about. Pick a small niche like hiking, kayaking, being a dad, running, knitting, having a cat, reading—anything. Think of this like the old evangelism method revolving around interest-based groups. Now it is happening online. Once you have picked your interest, either create a private visible Group, or you can join a local community Group that has already been created.

If you decide to create a Group, find ten of your friends and tell them that you are creating a Facebook Group to foster relationships in the community that will hopefully lead to gospel conversations. Ask those ten friends to invite ten of their friends, and now Facebook's algorithm will pick up that it is a popular Group in your community and start sharing it with others on the sidebar "Suggested Groups."

When you create a Group, you have to create content to fill that Group, so create a weekly posting strategy. If you have a hiking Group, maybe every Monday you ask for a new hiking picture. Then just start sharing hiking tips, maps, and resources. When you have created an online community, you can move it offline by creating an Event in the Group for a meetup. For example, go hiking with your Group. Create relationships that move from online to offline to share the gospel through your life. Life change happens in the context of relationships.

Community is where we as Christians thrive. Right now, online communities are thriving. Facebook provides an incredible platform for online communities, especially for churches. Facebook Groups are great places to communicate about shared interests. You can create Facebook Groups for anything. For example, create specific Groups for every small group that your church has. Create a Group for your Men's Sunday School class or for Youth Moms. The opportunities you have with Groups are endless.

Ads

Organizations and churches can use Facebook Ads to help them connect with their communities and achieve their goals. You can spend whatever you wish and get as specific as you like about whom you want to reach.

If you are ready to start running ads, open your church's Page on your computer and click the blue button in the lower-left corner that says "Promote." You could also go to facebook.com/ads, and then click "Create an Ad." Next, decide what you want your ad to help you do. Let's say Easter is coming up, and you want to get more people to check out the Easter Sunday information on your website. First, choose "Get More Website Visitors."

Second, add images and text for your ad. This is often referred to as your "ad creative." Facebook will suggest a picture and text, but feel free to change them. If you are advertising the upcoming Easter Sunday, a picture of one of your church members might be better than a picture of your church's building, for example. Your text should be concise, simple, and catchy. You can use emojis or make a list to better communicate certain points. If you are advertising a link, it is important to set an open graph image on your website. An open graph image is an image that is shared and made large when you share a link on Facebook. You can change that image and set it.

The third step is to create an audience. Tell Facebook whom you want to reach. People over the age of eighteen who live in the local area and up to twenty miles around the church's zip code might make a good audience for Easter Sunday. You can add those details and many more. Another great way to create an audience is to upload your church's email list and then create a "lookalike" audience. This will target people similar to the people who are on your church's list—perhaps their friends and families—which is a great place to get started.

You may want to get in touch with people within ten miles of the church since it often has a physical location. If your church has a strong online presence, maybe you'll want to reach out to a wider audience, like a whole city.

Your final step is to set your budget. The best part about creating Facebook ads is that even a modest budget can go a long way. Tell Facebook how long you want your ad to run and how much you would like to spend. You will never be billed more than the budget you set, and you can even see an estimate of how many people are likely to view your ad. Then, choose how you want to pay.

Once you have submitted your ad, it will be reviewed to ensure that it does not violate any of Facebook's advertising policies, a process that can take twelve to twenty-four hours. If it is approved, it should start running. If you do not like the results, you can edit or pause your ad.

Facebook ads are designed to help you reach your church's goals and connect with your community. They are quick to implement and easy to update. You can set a budget of how much you would like to spend and connect with prospective church members quickly and easily.

Instagram

According to TechCrunch.com, "After months of testing, Instagram launched on Oct. 06, 2010. Systrom and Krieger [the creators of Instagram] didn't know exactly what to expect, but 25,000 users showed up on the first day. For late 2010 when there were fewer iPhones on the market, that was a big number . . . Instagram hit one million users in three months. Then that became two million, which then became

10 million users. Unlike many apps at the top of the charts, Instagram didn't have to spend a dime to get where it was. It was organic growth."[21]

Instagram has become a widely used social media app, with millions of users. It is an effective way for churches to stay relevant in today's world. This is especially important because millennials are more likely to turn to social media when looking for information about their faith or church.

Additionally, churches can use Instagram effectively as a tool for evangelism. The Apostle Paul used stories about Jesus to share the gospel message in his day. Similarly, churches can use Instagram posts and stories to share the gospel with their followers. This can be a powerful way to connect with people and grow congregations. Ultimately, Instagram can be a valuable tool for churches to use in order to stay relevant, connect with younger generations, and share the gospel of Jesus Christ.

Instagram Demographics

Different social platforms have different target demographics. Instagram users are composed of 510 million females and 490 million males. One hundred thirty million Instagram users reside in the United States, with 89 percent of users living outside the United States. Recent data collected conclude that 293 million global Instagram users are 18 to 24 years of age, while 338 million are between 25 and 34.[22]

One of the most intriguing demographic studies of Instagram shows that 72 percent of teens across the globe use Instagram, and 73 percent of teens residing in the United States say Instagram is the best way for brands to reach them.[23] Let that sink in: nearly three-fourths of US teens say Instagram is the best way for brands, which in your case is your church, to reach them. What does that mean for your youth group? College group? Your church?

With Instagram having more features than just its initial photo-sharing to keep up with other social apps, some churches are making full-force efforts and are being repaid with online engagement and

---

[21] Cutler, Kim-Mai, "From 0 To $1 Billion In Two Years: Instagram's Rose-Tinted Ride To Glory," TechCrunch, April 9, 2012, https://techcrunch.com/2012/04/09/instagram-story-facebook-acquisition/.

[22] "Instagram by the Numbers: Stats, Demographics, and Fun Facts," Omnicore, accessed March 22, 2021, https://www.omnicoreagency.com/instagram-statistics.

[23] "Instagram by the Numbers."

brand awareness. For example, an unnamed church in Florida is a multicampus church with an Instagram following of more than 12,000 people. What sets this church apart is how they approach Instagram Stories (short, fifteen-second video clips or pictures that stay on a user's profile for twenty-four hours). Showcasing different campuses and campus pastors with "Instagram Takeovers," highlighting volunteers with "Meet the Team" clips, and sharing member-posted content all boost community feeling. People connect with people, and this church sets the standard of using Instagram Stories to connect with people.

The notion that people connect with people is supported by the fact that some of the church's most engaging content is not a picture of the pastor preaching or a Sunday recap video. It is the story of a real person. Covenant of Love Church (@myclchurch) shared a post recapping a spontaneous healing that broke out in one of their services. From that post, the church's engagement soared, not necessarily with the number of likes but with people directly messaging the church on how they were changed.[24] People connected to the story in the picture, which allowed them to share their own experiences. Giving people the ability at their fingertips to share their lives with your church is one of the most significant advantages of Instagram.

Building an Instagram Plan for Your Church

Just like with all good things in life, you need a plan to succeed. First, if you do not have an Instagram account, you should create one. It can be done easily by downloading the app and following the prompts. When setting up your Instagram, be mindful in choosing your username. Consider using not only your church name or acronym but also your location. The key is to make it easily searchable and identifiable. Set up your Instagram account as a business account so you can connect it with your church's Facebook Page. You can also schedule content via Facebook's Creator Studio if connected correctly.

The next step is creating your profile biography, or bio. With Instagram's minimalist design, you only have 150 characters to attract attention. It is essential that your bio be chock-full of information. Take the most flavorful adjectives that describe your church's personality and vision, and make them key statements in your bio. End your bio with a call

---

[24] Katie Allred and Kenny Jahng, *Instagram Posts That Worked: Real-Life Examples from Church Communicators across the Country* (self-pub., Amazon.com, 2020), 23–24.

to action such as, "Watch our latest service," "Listen to our podcast," or "Need prayer? Message us." You can also add your church's website or use a service like LinkinBio or LinkTree to share links later.

Now that you have created your account and written a great bio, it is time to start posting. Consistency is key when it comes to strategizing your posting plan. While some churches may have enough content to post one or two times a day, realistically, your church may only have enough content for three to four times a week. Quality is better than quantity. Ensure what you are posting is intended for your target audience, is engaging, and has a purpose.

Some posts that generally do well are Bible verse graphics, Sunday recaps, and pictures of people enjoying your church's community. Highlight special moments, ask volunteers for their stories, or tell stories about congregation members. Building a great Instagram feed is about more than just pretty pictures. It is about sharing the story of your church and the people who make it a community.

Besides feed posts, Instagram has Instagram Stories and, more recently, a Reels feature that rivals other social apps such as Snapchat and TikTok. With Instagram Stories, it is easy to do short daily encouragements or mini devotionals. It is also a useful tool to showcase in-the-moment events or Sunday services.

Instagram is a viable and growing social media platform that churches should be aware of and become a part of. Remember to be consistent in posting; consistent and clear content will help your church reach its goals.

YouTube

YouTube is the most effective tool to help church leaders reach more people so they can change more lives.
—Dave Adamson, Online Pastor at Northpoint Ministries

YouTube has over two billion active users, but many churches do not treat it as a social channel.[25] For the church, it has become a free video

---

[25] "YouTube," YouTube, accessed March 22, 2021, https://www.youtube.com/intl/en-GB/about.

archive where we stuff away Sunday mornings to never be seen or heard from again. But what if there is a better way?

YouTube is the world's second-largest search engine,[26] yet churches do not take advantage of this platform. We often name our sermon videos with titles such as the date and expect that only our congregation would want to watch it. We should stop thinking of YouTube as a repository for our dead content and think of it as a place for us to have conversations with those far from Christ.

Google, the world's largest search engine, owns YouTube. They want to show local answers first for questions when people search, but more often than not, there's not a local answer to "How can I pray?" or "What happens after I die?" So these seekers get sent to the next best place, but it is not your church. We should be creating content so they get sent to your church.

What questions did you have before you came to know the Lord? Did you Google these questions? Today's kids, teens, and adults alike are going online to figure out their theology. The question is, where is your church online? Where is your church on YouTube? It is much more comfortable for a teen or adult to search these questions on their own and in their safe space with no audience to be shocked by their question. Does your church have an answer to the questions they are asking? Churches should create content that compels viewers to want to learn more about Jesus and shares with them the gospel hope each time. So how can you do this?

First, resurrect that old video content. Most of your sermon library has great-quality content for viewers who are far from Christ; they just do not know how to access it. Renaming old sermons with more topical titles is a great place to start. Most churches fall into the rut of naming their sermon content something like, "January 19, 2020 | West End Baptist Church." This fails to tell the user what the sermon is about. Give context in the title to engage new viewers who are searching for what you have to offer. You have it in the sermon video, so why not advertise that in the title? You never see a book cover with the date it was written, the author's town, and nothing else. You see a compelling, all-encompassing title about the theme of the book. Every sermon has a theme; use it to

---

[26] Alexander Gould, "Don't Overlook the Second Largest Search Engine Anymore," *Longview News-Journal,* January 24, 2014, https://www.news-journal.com/news/local/dont-overlook-the-second-largest-search-engine-anymore/article_fb9fbc34-3874-597c-a68f-c527037619fd.html.

hook the audience. Then it is the sermon and pastor's job to engage the audience.

Second, make a plan to strategically create content around questions and specific keywords. Google Ads offers a great resource—the keyword research tool—that allows you to see what keywords are most popular when people are searching for things like your organization or church. For example, when people are searching for a boutique, they most commonly search for "fashion retailer" or "boutique." As a small boutique owner, using those keywords in your text will help generate your store as a result, even if your business name does not have the keyword in the name (e.g., "New Thread Co."). Find out what are the most commonly searched-for words, phrases, and questions in your area, and use those words in your text.

Google Trends is a great resource a church can leverage to assure its online content has the best chance to be seen by those searching for what it has to offer. Google Trends is a place where you can see what keywords are most commonly used when discussing a certain topic, where the most inflation is in the country about different searches, and more. To give you context, find the Google Trends Annual Report of 2019 by going to https://trends.google.com/trends/yis/2019/US/ or searching "Google Trends Annual Report 2019." You can see that 2019 was a big year in the Google search engine for Disney+, farmhouse decor, Avengers, and the Washington Nationals, and that people were most interested in learning how to make a shepherd's pie in the recipe department. That's neat. Let's make it applicable to the church. In the United States in 2020, the town of Sioux Falls, South Dakota, had the highest search results for "churches." It can get that specific! So how can you use this to help reach people who are searching for the gospel? Get on Google Trends, do the homework, and see what keywords are trending in your area or just in general, and use those keywords in titles and descriptions of your YouTube Videos. Put them in your bio, in posts, and anywhere else it would make sense. This will generate traction for your sites and videos, bringing the gospel to reach larger audiences through your organization.

Third, we should partner with other YouTubers with larger audiences. This works in corporate advertising efforts all the time, so why not apply it to the church world and gain the same success with spreading the good news? The outcome desired can be scaled simply by looking at the follower count the YouTuber has. If you are a smaller church, contacting a YouTuber with 3.4 million worldwide subscribers might not be the best bang for your buck here. Find a local YouTuber with a following that aligns with your church and its size. Figure out what you would like from them. If they have a large YouTube following, you can sponsor a video of theirs where they talk about topics applicable to your church. Or, if they have a large Instagram account, they can promote your livestream or YouTube channel on their social media. Just because their main platform is YouTube, that does not mean they do not have a large audience on other social media platforms as well. Often, cross-promotional advertising is expected as part of a contract. Find the YouTubers you would like to promote your content and in what ways, create a contract, and contact either them or their management team. Part of this contract should include links to your church's website, YouTube channel, social media accounts, and so on. Once a video is posted that you are tied in to, manage the comment section for questions or concerns regarding your involvement.

We live in a digital and social world, so use that opportunity to spread the gospel through your church. Implement smart search strategies and strategic partnerships to stretch your church's reach online. YouTube is a great social media platform, and this is just a small portion of what can be done to reach others with it.[27]

Twitter

Twitter was originally created for microblogging, or short-form blogs. Originally, the user could only post 140 characters, which kept the content very brief. Today, a post allows for twice the number of characters, 280, and allows users to thread their own conversations by replying to their previous post, therefore making a much longer and detailed post that is easy to follow. Twitter also has "fleets," which are their own version of "stories" like many other platforms.

Should your church be on Twitter? For many businesses, Twitter exists as a platform for handling customer service requests. For many authors, celebrities, and even pastors, Twitter exists to connect and communicate with their wider audience. For churches, it depends entirely on your church's size, reach, and preference. If you are at a megachurch, you should probably have some kind of a presence on

---

[27] Gould, "Don't Overlook the Second Largest Search Engine Anymore."

Twitter. If you are a smaller church, you should consider if your congregation uses Twitter through a survey. Many churches have a Twitter handle and do not use it. They just save their name so they have it if in the future more of their congregation members begin to use it. Again, the question is, "Where is your target audience?" If the answer is that they are on Twitter, you should probably join and use Twitter.

Another note on Twitter: many pastors use Twitter as a sort of "bullhorn." This should be used carefully. Also be sure to check and double-check what your pastor is "liking" or "favoriting" on any social media platform; it could come back to haunt them and you.

Other Social Media Platforms

There are hundreds of social media platforms on the Internet. Should your church be on all of them? No. Should your church be on some of them? Maybe. The answer really lies in your target audience—your church members and the people you are trying to reach.

To understand which social media platforms are best for your target audience, seek to understand what each platform was created for and what it has since become. The good news is you do not need to be on them all. It actually can hurt your organization or church to be sprawled out everywhere on the Internet. If you are always trying to crank out content specialized to each platform, it likely will not be as high quality as it would be if you stuck to a few and did those well.

Recall that social media is free marketing that you control, but it is only useful if done correctly. Find the platforms that give your accounts the highest return on investment, or ROI (variables include the effort and resources it takes to create your content and the interaction rate), and use those as much as possible. It is not about getting the most followers; it is about influencing the right followers. You can have a million followers, but if your interaction rates are low, there's no point.

One social media platform that took 2020 by storm is TikTok. TikTok is a video platform full of short videos, only lasting up to a minute. It has an intuitive video editing app built in with fun songs and effects. The "For You" page has helped make thousands of people "TikTok famous" and helps curate videos and users for you through your preferences of how fast the user skips previous content or stays and engages by "hearting," commenting, or following that user.

TikTok was controversial for a while because it is a Chinese company. President Trump approved an executive order to halt transactions on TikTok, as well as on WeChat, on August 6, 2020.[28] Eventually, TikTok announced a deal with Oracle and Walmart to keep the app open in the United States, CNBC reported.[29]

Now that TikTok is not going anywhere and is gaining an "average 14 new users every second," we should carefully consider if this is a good platform for churches.[30] If your target audience is young, like a student ministry, and you find through a survey of your student ministry that many of your students are using TikTok, it might make sense to join. If your congregation is older and does not use social media, it would not make as much sense to join.

Snapchat is one of the most infamous social media platforms of them all. Snapchat is a platform where you can send text messages, photos, and videos, and they automatically disappear after some time. Opinions have fluctuated on whether the platform is worth pursuing for churches. It was notoriously known as a "sexting" platform for a while, and many parents were worried about their children joining. However, that did not really stop teens; 48 percent of users are 15- to 25-year-olds.[31]

Whether you use Snapchat for your church depends on your congregation and the trust you have in the person running that account. Many larger churches created Snapchat accounts and have all but abandoned the platform for newer platforms with more metrics and fewer concerns over privacy and sexualization.

Another possible platform for churches to consider is LinkedIn. LinkedIn is owned by Microsoft, and it is primarily considered to be a professional social networking site. Many people use LinkedIn to showcase their resumes and accomplishments. LinkedIn allows for

---

[28] Wilbur Ross, "Commerce Department Prohibits WeChat and TikTok Transactions to Protect the National Security of the United States," Street Insider, September 18, 2020, https://www.streetinsider.com/Mergers+and+Acquisitions/Commerce+Department+Prohibits+WeChat+and+TikTok+Transactions+to+Protect+the+National+Security+of+the+United+States/17372727.html.

[29] Steve Kovach, "TikTok Deal Puts U.S. Owners in Charge, but Chinese Parent Company Still Has Some Say," CNBC, September 21, 2020, https://www.cnbc.com/2020/09/21/tiktok-deal-splits-control-between-us-and-chinese-owners.html.

[30] "Global Social Media Stats," DataReportal, accessed September 25, 2021, https://datareportal.com/social-media-users.

[31] H. Tankovska, "U.S. Snapchat Usage by Age 2020," Statista, January 28, 2021, https://www.statista.com/statistics/814300/snapchat-users-in-the-united-states-by-age.

posting, reacting, commenting, and even "stories" like many other platforms already discussed. The difference between LinkedIn and Facebook is that Facebook is about personal connections, while LinkedIn is for business networking.

If your church is primarily made up of professionals, it might make sense to create a church page so they can receive their church news and updates there. The kind of content you might share on LinkedIn would differ from what you share on Facebook. LinkedIn content for churches might be building updates, ministry updates, and things that would matter from an executive level.

There will always be a new platform to explore online. When deciding whether your church should be on it, remember to always ask yourself, "Is this where my target audience is?" and then follow that up with facts and data by surveying and some preliminary research. You might be surprised by what platform your church really is using, and it can help guide you toward using the platform that is most relevant to your church as a whole.

In social media, we should aim for growth, but interaction and engagement is far more important. For example, if you have a thriving student ministry, spending a lot of time and resources on TikTok and Instagram would be beneficial. If your congregation is an older audience, Facebook and email might be the right choices, but not TikTok. Find where your audience is, and pour into that. Do more by doing less, well.

Social Media Policy

Does my church really need a social media policy? Just as most places of business and churches have standards of conduct for employees in the real world, we need to also have clear expectations for our staff's online interactions. Not only do our posts, comments, and photos reflect the churches where we serve, but more importantly, as Christians, our social media profiles represent Christ in this world.

As staff members of churches, we have an opportunity to model what it means to live out our lives as Christ-followers to our congregations, friends, and communities. That said, many people do not spend as much time contemplating their comments online, and most discipleship tools fail to address online friendships and relationships when instructing on how to share the love of Christ with others. Giving your staff some guidelines in a social media policy can help them be more mindful of their role as representatives of your church and the church as a whole, which, in turn, can have a positive influence on others.

Social media has shifted the way we communicate with one another. Even though the method has changed, we are still called to follow Christ's example when communicating with others. Having guidelines that remind us to be gracious, encouraging, and truth-filled in our responses and interactions with others online is necessary to keep us focused on the reason we communicate with others in the first place: to share the love of Christ and to make disciples.

As Christians, we are called to live for Christ in all that we do and say, and that includes our use of social media. Brady Shearer of ProChurchTools says:

> What does the Bible say about social media? And should churches even be using social [media] in the first place? Perhaps you've encountered resistance in the past from senior leadership on the topic of social media because they're uncertain how it aligns with the mission of a church. For my part, I look to The Great Commission. Jesus said, "Therefore go and make disciples of all nations" [Matt 28:19]. So the mandate here is to be where the people are. And social checks that box.[32]

Keep in mind a few principles when you are developing a social media policy. Be clear and specific. Clarify why the church needs a policy. Your policy should be very specific as to what the church's staff can and cannot do on social media. Your social media policy should reflect your mission and values and outline the appropriate use of social media platforms.

The church's social media policy should include examples to illustrate the church's expectations for each guideline. You can do some brainstorming to decide collectively on the appropriate use of social platforms.

Leaders of the church ought to determine how social media will be monitored by their staff and what consequences will result when staffers fail to follow the guidelines. An excellent policy for social media is useless if the church does not enforce it. Make a decision on

---

[32] Brady Shearer, "Social Media Policy for Churches: The Definitive Guide," *Nucleus* (blog), September 1, 2020, https://www.nucleus.church/blog/social-media-policy-churches.

whether monitoring is necessary. If so, who will do that? What happens if something is reported? What is the process for addressing the concern? If it is decided that a mistake was made, how will the staff handle it? By making these decisions now, church leadership staff will know what to do in case of a crisis situation online.

Develop team members as "digital disciples." Your most important role is to help them see social media as a field of mission—an opportunity to share God's grace with people. Phil Schneider's *The Social Christian: A Theological Exploration of Social Media* examines several problems encountered by Christians when engaging on social media. He urges Christians to bear the banner of Christ and share it with others.

In conclusion, the social media policy cannot and should not be created in a vacuum. Seek insight from a group of church members, church staff, members of the business community, and social network experts to craft a policy that is relevant and effective and that will serve your church's mission.

Social Media Case Study: Redemption Church (Beaumont, Texas)

By Derek Hanson

One of the trickier parts of social media is figuring out how to reach your own church while at the same time offering content that can reach people beyond your immediate following. It is difficult to maintain a consistent message and visual identity, and refrain from making social posts that are just announcements for events coming up at your church. You want to remain fresh and relevant, you want your content to stand out in people's social feeds, and you want to offer content that speaks to people in a deep and engaging way. So every post cannot be so consistent that it becomes stale or rote.

Great church social media can find the right combination of brand consistency across single and multiple social media platforms, create visually compelling posts using a variety of design strategies, and bring relevant content that keeps the gospel at its core while also taking on tough social topics. Redemption Church in Beaumont, Texas, has figured out how to do all of these.

Photos Are Brand Consistent

When you think about brand consistency on social media, you might think that means every post should include the church's logo. However, a brand is more than just a logo (see chapter 2 on branding); it is the story of your church and how others see you. When you scroll through Redemption's Instagram feed, for instance, it is easy to see the visual consistency in every post. How do they do that, and why does it appear to be on brand?

Redemption's social media posts incorporate a balance of photography, video, and graphic design. How you can tell that there is brand consistency across each of these communication genres is subtle but striking when you take a more analytical look. Each photograph is completely unique in that they capture different people, on different days, and in different locations. What makes them consistent is the quality of photography is very good, shots of people are composed the same way, and the tone of the subjects in each photo is similar.

Take a look at these three photos. [33] Each one has two subjects embracing each other, facing the camera directly, and smiling. The photos are brand consistent

---

[33] Permission to reprint images granted by Byron Ellis, pastor, Redemption Church, via email, March 23, 2021.

because they visually represent part of the vision of Redemption Church, where "every man, woman, and child experiences life-change through Jesus," because the church is an "authentic community where no matter where you are at in following Jesus, you are welcomed, loved, and cared for."[34]

Any photo of church members shared by Redemption features happy and welcoming people, and the colors are bright and warm. To further enhance the consistency in Redemption's social media feed, each photo is color graded the same based on the purpose. If you follow Redemption Church on Instagram, you will know immediately when you see a photo from them without even seeing a logo.

Photos Are Visually Compelling

To create a visually compelling Instagram feed, though, you cannot have every image and every post precisely the same. Repeat equals defeat. As we see the photos of people engaging with the camera, bringing joy and life to followers, Redemption's image covers for IGTV posts show lead pastor Byron Ellis engaging with the congregation. The photo composition keeps Pastor Ellis framed in the center, the camera is slightly positioned to point up at the subject, and he is never facing the camera directly. Each image of Pastor Ellis captures a teaching moment on the stage, and the color is darkened to bring the mood of the worship venue.

What is the purpose of creating a photograph in this style and tone that is starkly contrasted to

---

[34] "Vision and Values," Redemption Church, Beaumont, TX, accessed March 22, 2021, https://www.redemptiontx.com/vision.

the other photos in Redemption's Instagram feed? By changing the photographic technique, not only are they creating contrast in their social feed, but they are also compelling their audience to engage with the content. The photographer has composed an image that places the social media follower in a chair with the rest of the congregation. Each photo captures a live moment of Pastor Ellis's teaching, bringing motion and interaction with an in-person audience that compels the Instagram viewer to click the post and watch the video. At that moment, you are transported into the venue with the rest of the congregation to hear expositional preaching, which is another core value of Redemption Church.

While Redemption's Instagram feed is visually compelling because of its balanced use of great photography and videos, they also incorporate graphic design elements into posts that speak to relevant social issues.

Social Posts That Matter to People

Throughout Redemption's Instagram feed, you find a great mixture of photographs, videos, and graphics. The graphics stand out not just because they are well designed; they stand out because they speak to relevant cultural and social issues that tie into their sermons *and* stand alone as great teachable moments. Check out part of their Instagram profile grid. A series of typographic designs surrounds the great photos. Each graphic features bright, bold colors that contrast the muted, warm tones of the photos. Visually, this captures the audience's attention and sets each post apart from the others while keeping a similar aesthetic. Now, engage with the content, and each post in the series pictured here shares a minimessage about marriage. If you go to Redemption Church or watch their sermons, you will see a clear connection to the teaching from Pastor Ellis on the Song of Solomon. The content serves the congregation as an extension of the Sunday services and reinforces the concepts from the sermons.

If you happen to follow or find Redemption's Instagram page and do not attend their Sunday services, the content is still relevant and stands on its own. You do not have to attend church to learn that "Marriage is not 50-50 but 100-100." Redemption's posts are culturally relevant because they feature a topic that speaks to people universally while sharing the gospel.

Redemption Church is a relatively small church, with only 300 attendees, but they have more than 4,800 followers on their Instagram account. They attract a broader following by maintaining a consistent, authentic brand; curating visually compelling posts; and offering relevant content. All these things work together in unison—the holy trinity of social media. Redemption Church is a great example to follow on social media.

Questions

1. Of the three characteristics in this social media case study on Redemption Church, which is the most important for churches to follow? Why?
2. You just started as the communication director at a church that has not invested much time or energy into its Instagram

account because it does not think social media is important. Taking what you learned from Redemption Church, how would you convince your lead pastor and leadership to start investing resources into Instagram?

3. Find three other churches with a comparable Instagram following and demographic to Redemption Church. Analyze their Instagram feeds. Do you see some of the same strategies Redemption Church uses? What is similar? What is different? What can you learn from looking at other churches' Instagram accounts?

Chapter 5

Websites

G rab your phone and Google "church near me." Do you find your church? What types of churches do you find? What impressions do you have before you even read a word?

Click through to the first few church websites you find. By visiting these different websites, you can probably guess which churches are more established and what kind of worship they observe (e.g., traditional or contemporary). You can tell if these websites have been updated recently or if they leave something to be desired. We know churches are about more than websites, but if it weren't for online meetings or livestreaming from church websites during the COVID-19 pandemic, many of us would not have been able to have church.

Why should you have a church website? When people search for your church online, what do they find? Can they find you at all? When people click through to your website, is it clear that you are a church? Where and when do you meet? What does your church believe?

Church websites are not just important, they are necessary. They are often the first communication asset a seeker finds when searching for a church or the answer to a theological question online. A well-designed website communicates that the church takes itself seriously. Church websites should not be known for bad font choices and outdated designs. The first reason your church needs a website is because discovery happens online.

Think about the last time you moved. I moved recently. When I needed a new gym, what did I do? I went online and searched for a gym near me. Same for a church. I researched churches in my area, read reviews online, and visited many church websites to read about their beliefs, denominations, and staff members, and to make my own assumptions about what they valued via what they showed me on their website.

A 2018 Pew Research study stated 96 percent of people rely on their own research when making an important decision, and 46 percent explained that they rely on digital tools, or the Internet.[1] Their research found that the Internet was "a starting point but often not the endpoint":

> I rely on information on the internet, e.g., a move to another city made me look up geographical information, cost of living, and also info from residents of the new area and also input from friends of long standing, using their experiences.
> —Woman, 77

> If I were to change jobs, enter college, etc., I would conduct research on the internet. I would search for news articles, seek out publications that evaluate the choices, and try to talk directly to experts or people with relevant experiences.
> —Man, 54.[2]

Another interesting fact is that 46 percent of all Google searches are local. Nearly 50 percent of web traffic is people searching for places, locations, and groups near them.[3] Church websites play a vital role in creating awareness that the church exists. If someone cannot find your church on Google, then it does not exist to them.

---

[1] Erica Turner and Lee Rainie, "Most Americans Rely on Their Own Research to Make Big Decisions, and That Often Means Online Searches," Pew Research Center, March 5, 2020, https://www.pewresearch.org/fact-tank/2020/03/05/most-americans-rely-on-their-own-research -to-make-big-decisions-and-that-often-means-online-searches.

[2] Turner and Rainie, "Most Americans Rely on Their Own Research."

[3] Lindsay Kolowich Cox, "16 Stats That Prove the Importance of Local SEO," HubSpot Blog, June 25, 2019, https://blog.hubspot.com/marketing/local-seo-stats.

Pastors are going online too: "In 2000, just over eight in 10 pastors said they used a computer at church (83%). Today nearly all pastors do (96%)," according to Barna Research in 2015.[4] That same research states:

More than half of pastors today agree that the Internet is a powerful tool for effective ministry (54%, up from 35% in 2000). A similar percentage say that for a church to be effective in the future, it will need to have a significant website or presence on the Internet (55%). Additionally, more than half of pastors agree that developing a significant presence on the Internet is a good investment of their church's money (54%).[5]

So yes, people, including pastors, are using the Internet to make all kinds of decisions. But why else should you have a website? A website helps keep your congregation active and engaged. According to research, "64% of church goers say the church website is important in facilitating participation in church."[6] Another reason to have a church website is that your church controls it; it is a form of "owned media," which means you or your church owns the platform, no one else.

Not only does your church's website help people find you and help to keep your congregation engaged, but a website can also show your church's community involvement. A church website can be a great place to showcase stories of life change in your church. It can also be a great place to have written devotionals and showcase other talents of your congregation.

Finally, a church needs a website for charitable giving, which has gone online. Sixty percent of all tithes are given to the church digitally, and churches that accept tithing online increase their overall donations by 32 percent—that is not a small number.[7] If you already have a website, I would consider these questions from Pastor Brandon Cox about your church's website:

---

[4] "Cyber Church: Pastors and the Internet," Barna Group, February 11, 2015, https://www.barna.com/research/cyber-church-pastors-and-the-internet.

[5] "Cyber Church: Pastors and the Internet."

[6] Jerod Clark, "Church Website Statistics," The Network, August 1, 2012, https://network.crcna.org/church-web/church-website-statistics.

[7] "Church and Religious Charitable Giving Statistics," Nonprofits Source, 2020, https://nonprofitssource.com/online-giving-statistics/church-giving.

- Is our website responsive and mobile-friendly?
- Is our most basic information easy to find on our main homepage (location, service times, etc.)?
- Do we use imagery that tells people we're human, we're alive, and we're welcoming?
- Are event listings available and up to date?
- Can people easily know what we believe, what we value, and how we function as a church?
- Do we have links to our Facebook Page and other social profiles on our website?
- Is there a way for people to reach out and get in touch with us without leaving our website?
- Can people easily know how to pursue next steps such as baptism, joining a small group, or volunteering in an area of ministry?
- Do we have a page dedicated to our staff and/or key leaders so potential visitors can know who we are?[8]

How to Make a Church Website

There are many ways to create a church website. You can hire a company or a person. You can build it yourself using CSS/HTML. You can use a builder like Wix or SquareSpace, or you can use a host like FlyWheel, install WordPress, and then use a theme like Divi or Hello Elementor with the Elementor plugin.

There are three options that I recommend to most churches: hire a developer, use a website builder, or build the website on WordPress. Let's break down the different ways and consider some pros and cons of each way.

Hiring a Developer or Designer

I will almost always recommend hiring a company or a person to help build your website if you do not have such experience. For the time and effort it takes to build it yourself, you probably could have paid someone to do it—and do it better for less. The primary reason that

---

[8] Cox, "33 Questions" (see chap. 2, n. 6).

many churches do not hire a developer is cost. The cost can be prohibitive, but so can the costs of doing it wrong.

Pros of hiring a developer:

- They know what they are doing.
- They can guide you through the process.
- They can help you understand what is possible and what is not.
- They will save you time and possibly money.
- They will help you think of things you have not considered.
- They know more about search engine optimization.

Cons of hiring a developer:

- It is costly.

Using a Website Builder

Numerous website builders across the web can help you build a church website. You can use secular services like Wix or SquareSpace. You can also use a more church-focused website builder like The Church Co or Ministry Designs Omega Builder. Such editors are called "What You See Is What You Get," often shortened to WYSIWYG. A webpage can be designed with these editors using a graphical user interface. Users will be able to drag and drop HTML elements right onto the page while the editor codes the page. All these builders have their pros and cons as well.

Pros of using a website builder:

- They are cheap to get started.
- They are easy to use.
- They make maintenance easy.

Cons of using a website builder:

- They are hard to customize.
- They often look cookie cutter.
- Secular choices often leave church-specific tools like managing sermons or livestream out of their features.

Building a WordPress Site

Building a WordPress site is what I recommend to most churches. By this, I do not mean on WordPress.com. Wordpress.com is its own product, and while it might very well work for a church site, I recommend building a WordPress site on a host like WPEngine, FlyWheel, or Pressable. You can also purchase cheaper hosting at DreamHost, SiteGround, or BlueHost. Just remember that you get what you pay for. WordPress sites require hosting, a domain name purchase, a theme, and often plugins.

Pros of building a WordPress site:

- It is usually cheap to get started.
- You can build whatever you want.
- You are not limited to what builders can do design-wise.

Cons of building a WordPress site:

- Maintenance can be confusing.
- It is hard to customize.
- The number of options can be overwhelming to some people.
- It is easily hackable due to the large number of third-party plug-ins.

Churches can get free website hosting for WordPress and free email hosting through DreamHost with their 501(c)(3) documentation. Search for "DreamHost Nonprofit Discount" and find the article in their help section about it. Anyone can install WordPress for free on this host even though it does not say that directly on the site.

These three choices—having someone build, using a website builder, or using WordPress—are all good choices, and I recommend that you try out some form of each.

Important Things to Consider When Building a Website Regardless of Platform

Building a website can be an exciting process, but it's easy to get lost in the details and forget about some of the factors—for example, website speed, design, responsiveness, and security—that can have a big impact on your online success. It's important to keep these things in mind when building your site so you don't run into any unexpected problems down the road.

Website Speed

Website load speed is critical when designing and building a website. If the website does not load quickly, a user might leave. Also, search engines like Google will rank your website lower depending on your page speed. Peep Laja from CXL Optimization Agency stated:, "People make snap judgments. It takes only 1/10th of a second to form a first impression about a person. Websites are no different. It takes about 50 milliseconds (ms) (that's 0.05 seconds) for users to form an opinion about your website that determines whether they'll stay or leave."[9]

A simple way to help your site load quickly is to make sure all graphics and images are saved for "web and devices" through Photoshop or other graphic design software. This compresses them to a small file size and aids in website load times. Another website I recommend is BulkResizePhotos.com. You can upload your photos and it will quickly download your photos back to your computer compressed and ready for the web. What's also great about that website is that it's all done technically on your computer and while you are "uploading" them, they aren't being saved anywhere else on the web. It's all done in the browser and safely on your computer.

Design

The church website is often the primary way that many people interact with your church. Therefore, it is essential to make sure it looks professional and reflects well on your congregation. This section will cover best practices for designing a church website, including tips on organizing content, choosing fonts, and creating an attractive design.

Creativity is essential in web design, but so is conventionality. A church website should look professional and clean, so people pay attention to the content. A design that is too flashy or busy will distract visitors from the message you are trying to convey.

There are three main components of a site's navigation:

---

9 Peep Laja, "First Impressions Matter: Why Great Visual Design Is Essential," CXL, September 25, 2020, https://cxl.com/blog/first-impressions-matter-the-importance-of-great-visual-design.

- The header, which includes links for your homepage, about us page, contact information, etc.
- Secondary menus, where you can put links to pages like events, blog, etc.
- The footer, which typically includes copyright information, social media buttons, and other secondary items

It is essential for content on your website to be easy to find. A good way of organizing it is through a grid system. Creating this type of organization makes everything look more professional, and it is also easier for visitors to find the information they need.

The fonts you choose should be easy on the eyes and help convey your message. Using one type of font in all caps can be effective for headlines, so it stands out more, but if this is not legible or attractive, consider using different fonts. Do not use more than two or three fonts on your website.

A church website should be attractive but not distracting. When you design your site, pay attention to the way it looks: Is there too much going on? Does it look like a professional business or organization? You want people to read what you have written and learn about your congregation, so make sure that content is well organized in an easy-to-understand way.

MOBILE-FRIENDLINESS, OR RESPONSIVENESS

Have you ever been on a site where you had to zoom in and pinch the screen when on your mobile phone? When people say that a website is responsive or mobile-friendly, they mean that it is able to adapt its screen size to whatever device it is being displayed on. Optimize your website for mobile and desktop devices by creating a responsive design. This will help you get better rankings in search engines and increase the amount of time visitors spend on your site. Certain search engines, like Google, rank websites that are not mobile-friendly lower in searches.

SITE SECURITY

You will need to ensure your website can be secured with an SSL certificate wherever it is hosted. According to GlobalSign.com, SSL Certificates are small data files that digitally bind a cryptographic key to an organization's details. When installed on a web server, it activates the padlock and the HTTPS protocol and allows secure connections from a web server to a browser. Typically, SSL is used to secure credit card transactions, data transfer, and logins, and more recently is becoming the norm for secure browsing of social media sites.[10]

Google no longer endorses sites on their search engine that do not employ an SSL certificate. These are usually free and easy to install. Another security step you should take is to make sure your site is backed up daily. Many church websites have been lost because they did not have adequate backup. Finally, if you are using WordPress, you can also install security plug-ins like Sucuri or WordFence to help defend yourself against hackers.

Website Basics

Before you start building a website, you need to plan it first. But you cannot plan the website without first meeting with various members, pastors, and ministers to discover what they expect and need the church's website to do. You can then plan the following:

- Who will be in charge of maintaining and updating the website?
- How do you want to structure the content on your web pages?
- Do you want to have a blog on your website?
- What is the purpose of having a website at all, and what do you hope it will accomplish for your church?

It's also important that everyone involved knows how they can contribute. For example, if there are various ministry teams who need web pages, how can they update their own content?

The second step is to define your target audience. These are people who use the website. Knowing their general demographic background will help you design a website appropriate for them. Consider these questions: Who are the people who attend your church currently? What is the persona of your potential guest?

When designing a website, a designer should consider a few questions: Whom is this website for? What does the audience want and need to see or find? What is the next step we want a seeker or guest to take when visiting this page? We have already talked about the audience and personas in chapter 1. Pulling from your personas,

---

10 "What Is an SSL Certificate?," GlobalSign GMO Internet, Inc., October 22, 2020, https://www.globalsign.com/en/ssl-information-center/what-is-an-ssl-certificate.

you can probably lump people into two categories: seekers (people who are looking for a church) and church members. The purpose of a good church website is to outfit the people in both categories with the information they need to make decisions. Failing to provide adequate information in a logical and convenient manner can mean an inconvenience for a church member or the loss of a visit from a seeker; we do not want either.

The third step is to decide which content management system or website building platform to use. Use the information discussed earlier in this chapter to make a well-informed decision.

The fourth step is to gather content for your website. Many companies, people, and churches do not realize the amount of work it takes to gather the content necessary for a website launch. We will cover more about content in the section "What Should Be on a Church Website?"

The fifth step is to create a wireframe for your website. This is not a design; it is just a visual layout (usually in black and white) of where you want your content to be placed. You can even draw it on paper. This will help you visualize how and where you want your content to go and what other content needs to be created. This step is often skipped, and that is okay if you have a lot of experience. If you do not, or are dealing with a lot of information, I recommend wireframing at least your home page.

The sixth step entails creating a sitemap. A sitemap is a tool that helps you keep track of all pages on your website. So put together, it's easy for visitors to find what they are looking for without getting lost or going back out of their way! There are quite a few ways to organize a sitemap, but hierarchical is the easiest and best for most churches. Think of this as creating a "Ministries" page and having "Children, Students, Adults" listed underneath.

The seventh step is to plan the website's graphics. Church graphics are an essential part of the website design. They help people form their first impression of what it's all about, and can make them feel more connected with you as they browse through your site content. Remember to make sure graphics are saved for web usage to compress the file size for better load times. Graphics are a great way to make your church stand out from others in the community. They should be straightforward to read, with branding integrated into them as well. Contrast in graphics is important to make your graphics readable. For example, look at the Five Guys website.[11] The color red is incorporated throughout the website. By now, the church should already have an established brand. The church will need some kind of logo for a website, even if it is a type-only treatment.

The eighth step is to plan the website's navigation. What does the church want people to do on their website, and where do they want them to go? People usually just think of the primary navigation, but also consider the footer. In the website's primary navigation, try to limit the menu to six options, if possible. Examples of these options could be *About, New Here, Messages, Ministries* (with a drop-down of those ministries if necessary), Events, and Give. The fewer the options, the better. The fewer things people can do, the more likely they will do what you want them to do. If the web designer gives them too many options, they will not know what to do next. Notice what was not listed? The homepage. Homepages are typically linked in the logo area of the page in the top left-hand corner, so there is no need to link to the home page again in the menu bar.

The ninth step is to plan the website's typography and colors. The typography and colors of a website can make or break it. The typeface, font size, color treatment (backgrounds) are all factors in how users perceive the site—whether they find it attractive enough to stay on for long periods of time; thus creating an effective design with good readability levels across platforms like desktop computers and smartphones, etc. For example, red signifies love when used as branding globally but this may not always resonate locally—so be careful!

In the tenth step, web designers should consider accessibility. It is important to make pages accessible for those who are visually impaired as well as people with other disabilities. Web standards are developed and maintained by the World Wide Web Consortium (W3C). According to W3C, the goal of the web is to be accessible to all people, including those with a disability that limits their ability to perform computer tasks.[12] The Rehabilitation Act of 1973 prohibits discrimination against those with disabilities, and this applies to churches and

---

[11] "Five Guys," Five Guys, accessed September 2, 2021, http://www.fiveguys.com.

[12] "Introduction to Web Accessibility," Web Accessibility Initiative (WAI), accessed March 28, 2021, https://www.w3.org/WAI/fundamentals/accessibility-intro.

nonprofits.[13] WCAG 2.0 and 2.1 guidelines "are organized under 4 principles: perceivable, operable, understandable, and robust."[14]

The eleventh step is to start designing and gathering content. Web designers may start designing in Photoshop or Illustrator first or may start in the website builder. You can also just start with pen and paper. Remember to first wireframe or draw the preliminary website design to save time and effort when deciding where content will go. Additionally, content takes a lot of time to gather. Be sure to contact the right people to get the right information for the church's website.

Twelfth, and finally, is to plan for multiplatform displays. One of the most important criteria to consider when designing a website is how it will display on a number of different devices, including smartphones, tablets, and computers. Designing a church website takes time, but it is important that the designer accounts for different displays like iPhone, Android, laptops, even TVs in that design. If a website is not mobile-friendly, not only will people leave the website, Google and other search engines will actually rank the website lower.[15]

What Should Be on a Church Website

Your church website should provide information that visitors are looking for. A church website that makes it hard to locate addresses, times, and locations—critical information—is failing.

Many websites share common components such as the home page, an about page, and a contact page. Most church websites also include a staff listing page, a ministries page or pages about each ministry, and a page for sermons. One hallmark of a well-designed website is that its web pages have the same look and feel (i.e., the same layout, color scheme, typography, and style of graphics). Elements work the same way on each page. Most church websites include the following features:

- Audio of sermons

---

[13] "A Guide to Disability Rights Laws," Americans with Disabilities Act, accessed March 28, 2021, https://www.ada.gov/cguide.htm.

[14] "Web Content Accessibility Guidelines (WCAG) Overview," Web Accessibility Initiative (WAI), accessed March 28, 2021, https://www.w3.org/WAI/standards-guidelines/wcag.

[15] *Responsive Web Design with HTML 5 & CSS* by Jessica Minnick and *Web Development and Design Foundations with HTML5* by Terry Felke-Morris have more helpful information on how to design a website.

- Serving opportunities at the church
- Service information—times and directions
- Staff information
- Contact information
- A way for a visitor to plan a visit[16]

Good websites feature the following characteristics:

- Branding that is consistent throughout the website. The logo is clear and readable.
- The menu is accessible, and content can easily be found.
- The website has a search feature.
- Each web page includes a clear call to action.
- Each page has clear information "above the fold."
- The website includes breadcrumbs (navigation tool to help users know where they are on the website).
- Photography and video are used wisely and when it makes sense. There are more photos of people from the church than buildings.
- The footer should include service times and the church's address.

Homepage

A homepage is the first page users see when they access a website. Homepages should be designed primarily for visitors. The home page should have a clear call to action on how to get involved with your church immediately or receive more information. For example, include something like, "Sunday Morning Worship is at 11:00 a.m.," along with an address.

Your homepage should have clear information "above the fold," which means what loads first on the page before a user has to scroll. "Above the fold" is a newspaper term that refers to the content that is on the front page of the newspaper before you unfold it. Typically, that first headline would help sell papers that day and entice readers to read more. In the same way, you should create a "hero" image (a banner image) of worship or people in the community. This will be a large banner with your tagline and mission statement over it. Then create a call to action such as "Listen to the Latest Sermon."

---

[16] Jerod Clark, "Church Website Statistics," The Network, August 1, 2012, https://network.crcna.org/church-web/church-website-statistics.

Other sections of the homepage might include a feature on the latest sermon, a listing of upcoming events, and a little more information about the church. It is critical that service times and the church's address be located prominently on the home page. You could also include an email newsletter sign-up on the home page to increase your email list.

ABOUT US PAGE

The about us page, which is primarily for visitors, should clarify who your church is with the following information:

- Belief
- Mission and vision statements, as well as values
- Service times and the church's address
- Denominational information

Many churches include a staff page with a directory of their staff. These directories have plenty of pros and cons. They are often one of the most visited pages on a church website, but it might be for nefarious reasons; spam bots love to pull email addresses and phone numbers from these types of pages. Also, there is the question of privacy for your staff and their families. Each church staff will be different when it comes to this decision. If you do not include a staff listing, do include a feature on your senior pastor. People will be curious about leadership and their background. It is important to include some general information about your pastor and leadership, like executive pastors.

MINISTRIES PAGE(S)

Many church websites have one or many ministry pages. Churches can create pages for each ministry (e.g.,children, students, adults, or senior adults). When creating these pages, remember the 5Ws from chapter 1. You should list why these ministries exist, what they are, who directs these ministries, who can be involved, when the ministry meets or what events the ministry has, where the ministry meets, and how someone can get involved.

GIVING PAGE

The giving page should include a clear and easy path to online giving. There are multiple online giving solutions. If you would like to compare online giving solutions, check out givingfees.com. Use an online giving solution that makes setting up recurring giving easy for your church. You can either embed or link out to your giving "checkout" page. You should also include and explain all the possible ways to give, like by check, text, or any other means.

It is not only important to include a way to give but also to explain the why behind the giving. Be sure to include either a section or a page on why people should give and where the money goes. Helping people understand why will compel people to give more.

CONTACT PAGE

The contact page should include the church's address, mailing address (if different), phone number, fax number (if applicable), and an email address. You can also include a map or contact form.

Mobile Websites Versus Apps

Apps are trending as churches make decisions about what technology stack to use. A mobile app is an application that a user can download from the Apple App Store or Google Play Store. A mobile website works on any phone in a browser window like Safari or Google Chrome. The audience for a mobile app at a church is the congregation itself, whereas the audience for a website is primarily visitors, then church members. Many churches want apps and have apps, but the question remains if congregations should spend money on a mobile app if the church website is mobile-friendly.

Again, like anything else in marketing, what is the church's goal for having an app? Apps can be expensive and a lot to maintain going forward. A second question would be, can your app do anything that your current mobile-friendly website cannot?

Most church app companies provide typical features. Here's an example feature set:

- Bible
- A place to put sermon notes
- Deliver a livestream
- Host sermon video archives
- Push notifications
- Giving

A church website can do all these things except for push notifications; however, instead of push notifications, your church could use a texting service, like Text in Church, to send those notifications instead. Also, people tend to use and stick with the apps they are accustomed to using. For example, the Bible feature in the church app might be great, but some might like to keep all their notes on YouVersion apps to share with friends. A place to put sermon notes is also great but probably limited in searchability, unlike Apple Notes. YouTube live streams can be cast to various streaming devices on televisions, but does your app provider allow casting? Vimeo and YouTube are great for hosting video archives. Most app providers require you to have it there before manually importing each video's URL into their platform each week. Giving can be done on a mobile website in a short link (e.g., church. org/give) or through a giving provider with a text-to-give option. Also, churches can handle giving through Stripe or PayPal. Stripe and PayPal fees might be lower than your current online giving provider.

There are some new features offered by various app providers that provide more engagement within the app itself. Features like small group chat, creating an Alexa skill, and more are fresh and more in line with creating a mobile app that is not like a website. I do not think the tech is there yet; church apps are not as engaging as possible, but they will be one day.

Chapter 6

Advertising

It's not uncommon for church leaders to be hesitant at first when it comes to advertising their particular churches. Often they worry about how expensive and time-consuming it can be, but the benefits of advertising are more than worth any effort put into this venture. Church marketing is nothing like traditional forms of advertisement such as billboards or ads in local papers.

Simply put, advertising is when companies pay other companies money to advertise their products to potential customers. This could be via TV, Internet, magazines, or other media. Church advertising is when churches pay to advertise their church to the general public. People often confuse marketing with advertising, but advertising is the final P in the four Ps mentioned in chapter 1: promotion. It is also part of any integrated marketing communication plan.

In the church's case, an ad might be a focused message on why your church is different from other churches in the area. Church advertising can help people know about upcoming events and bring them in person to have an experience with God that they otherwise would not have had. Advertising also can show your community what the church is doing well by highlighting special events, recovery programs, and educational opportunities.

Where should churches advertise? A church can send an email to people in the local area if they have access to an email list through the chamber of commerce or other sources. Additionally, the church can do a direct mail piece. The church can also buy an ad in the local newspaper or on a local website, or it can have ads on billboards and in the phonebook. Today, many consider direct mail to be outdated. However, it can still be instrumental, especially when the church is trying to raise brand awareness to their local community or to tell people in the area about an upcoming outreach event. Advertising can also be done online, on Facebook, Google, and more.

Church advertising can be used to increase attendance, spread the gospel, or even raise funds. The church may want to consider how it advertises and its desired goal before selecting an advertisement. Church advertising allows people who are not in the local area or even the country to know about what the church is doing.

The first step when planning an ad campaign is to consider who your target audience is. This will entail doing market research and analyzing past marketing strategies that have been successful or unsuccessful in the area of your choice. A vital part of this process includes determining what types of people you want to attract. It also includes deciding which media outlets are best suited for campaign placement (e.g., radio stations versus newspapers).

The second step is to set a goal for the church's advertising. These goals should come from the church's overall marketing goals. Do you want this advertisement to inform, persuade, or remind people? You might create an informative ad to build brand awareness if you are a church plant. You might do a persuasive ad for a new outreach program like Celebrate Recovery. You could do an ad to remind the people in the community about the upcoming Easter service.

The third step is to determine the advertising budget and how much money should be allocated to various campaigns, such as print ads versus TV spots. It can be helpful to look at the church's budget to see what has been done in the past and decide what can be spent in the future.

After deciding on an overall goal for your campaign, determining a budget, and selecting which platforms are best suited for this particular advertisement type, the fourth step is to start creating the content of the advertisements. An ad needs to tell a story or convey a message. It can convey an inspirational message, an informative message, or even a persuasive one. You tell your story depending on the medium you choose to advertise on.

The fifth step is to select the medium in which your advertisement will appear. An ad on Facebook will be very different from an ad in Times Square, just like a direct mail piece will require different work than a video. For most churches just getting started with advertising, it is recommended to start with Facebook Ads because of their ease of use and free learning material through Facebook Blueprint.

The next step is to choose the best time and day for your advertisement. This includes deciding when you want it to start, how long it lasts each day, what days to run the advertisements, and so on. The ultimate goal is to balance frequency (how often you advertise) and reach (how many people see the ad).

Now, the final step: put it all together. Creating ads can be fun and challenging. It often takes a lot of creativity and skill to get your point across both creatively and succinctly. What kind of medium is used and the marketing goals of the church will determine how the advertisement is made. It is important not to let the team's creativity take away from the main message of the ad. Seek input from outsiders often; it is easy to get carried away.

Another factor to consider in any ad strategy is tracking the success of the ad campaign. For Facebook Ads, you can do this digitally through Facebook Ads Manager by tracking the number of impressions (total people who see the ad), clicks, and conversions. These are all important metrics to measure in order to improve future ads. If the ad is not fulfilling your marketing goals, you need to fix the ad. Maybe the medium is wrong. Maybe the copy needs to be changed. Maybe a video would be more effective. Use metrics to determine your next move.

Advertising is an essential tool for outreach and informing people about what your church has to offer, but churches often have limited budgets. Here are some ideas to advertise in creative ways: outreach events such as community-based activities like coffee with a pastor or building personal relationships by talking to members of other churches, producing YouTube videos, updating the church's Google My Business listing, blogging on the church's website, writing articles for local newspapers or magazine publications, and holding contests with prizes donated by companies outside of the congregation (which gives them exposure while bringing awareness inside the church walls too).

In conclusion, church advertising can be a beneficial tool that will bring people to your church and, hopefully, help them come to Christ. Many factors must be considered in any ad strategy, including the chosen advertising platform (medium) and marketing goals of the church. Advertising can be challenging to get right because it can be expensive and is very visible. However, many churches find that advertising campaigns are essential for bringing people into the congregation.

Chapter 7

Public Relations

The simplest definition of public relations (PR) is using media to create positive brand awareness and boost reputation. Sounds easy, right? If you have a plan in place and a solid understanding, it can be easy. Public relations is becoming one of the most popular forms of marketing and promotion. It can create "unwavering partnerships," which are important not only for business growth and sustainability but also for your church as it strives to grow, create, and connect with the community.[1]

Before focusing on the people you are targeting and building those connections with, you must first focus on your church and create a public relations strategy. The first step in developing a solid PR strategy is figuring out who the church is, what it does, whom it serves, and with whom in the community it wants to interact.

The backbone of PR is storytelling and effective dialogue—creating a narrative that people want to buy into. In this case, you are asking people to buy into not only the gospel but also the vision and mission of your church. Much like advertising and developing a marketing

---

[1] "About Public Relations," Public Relations Society of America, accessed March 17, 2021, https://www.prsa.org/about/all-about-pr.

strategy, first you must know your audience. Communicating effectively relies heavily on how your audience communicates. If you are trying to reach twenty somethings, you might use storytelling skills to create noteworthy and shareable Instagram content. If you are trying to reach senior citizens, you might take out an ad in the local newspaper with a well-written press release.

Next, create interesting and notable content. Figure out what works best for your church and your audience, then produce content they will want to share and with which they will engage. The United Methodist Church previously did an outstanding, relevant, and interesting campaign called "Rethink Church." Their core demographic was people ages eighteen to thirty-four. Instead of a normal push for attendance or "this is why you should choose our church," they engaged their target audience through social media and web-based interactions. Their hashtag #rethinkchurch has over 100,000 posts on Instagram alone.

Do something different. Do something creative. Do a fun community event, and invite local news stations. During the COVID-19 pandemic, many churches stepped up and helped their local communities. It was a great time to reach out to local news sources, bloggers, TV stations, and so on to let them know a church has resources and is willing to help the community. The Baptist Press featured this story: "The Send Relief ministry center in Kentucky has sent out supplies to assist other ministry centers across the nation, including 6,000 meals to New York City to provide for those under quarantine or are restricted to confinement in some way."[2] A story like this provides quite a bit of goodwill within the community, but no one outside the immediate church circle will know about it without a well-written press release that is picked up by local media outlets.

Writing a press release goes back to the backbone of PR: storytelling. Storytelling is making a narrative that people want to hear about in language that piques their interest. However, before writing a press release, you need to answer two important questions:

1. What angle of the story, event, or promotion is most interesting and newsworthy, not only to you but to your targeted demographic and prospective journalists?

[2] Brandon Elrod, "Southern Baptists Organize to Help Amid COVID-19 Crisis," Baptist Press, March 18, 2020, https://www.baptistpress.com/resource-library/news/southern-baptists-organize-to-help-amid-covid-19-crisis.

2. What do you hope this press release will achieve?

Once those two questions have been answered clearly and concisely, you can move on to actually writing the press release. A press release should typically be no more than 400 to 500 words in length and formatted with a 12-point to 14-point traditional font such as Arial or Times New Roman.

Next, write two or three sentences about what will happen during the event and whether the church will be handing anything out. After that, give information about how a person can register to attend the event. Include a point of contact for more information.

Finally, end with a short description of the church. This should include a brief history, vision or mission statement, and maybe a little bit about your pastors. When writing this section, think about what you would want to know about a church.

Now that you have your press release, gather a directory of local media outlets in your city, county, and adjacent cities. Include TV, radio, newspaper, and online-only publications. Contacting each of these media outlets will vary depending on the size of the city as well as the size of the stations and newspapers. Some helpful tips include:

- Television and local news stations typically have a direct line to contact their office and a directory to submit news on their website. Radio-locator.com is a great resource to figure out what radio stations are within your zip code. Once you know that, you can reach out to them individually.
- Submitting your press release to a newspaper involves emailing them your press release first. That might be to a certain journalist or in a general email. After the initial email is sent, follow up with a phone call. Journalists receive many stories and tips, so set yours apart by a personal follow-up.
- Pull the best parts of your press release and hit social media. Do not be afraid to tag local news stations or geo-tag where the event will take place. After you have a directory of local outlets, keep it on hand. Build relationships. Help them see the value your church has to offer to the community.

Here's a basic outline of how to write and format your own press release:[3]

FOR IMMEDIATE RELEASE

CONTACT: Contact Person, Phone Number

Email Address, Website URL

[Date]

[HEADLINE] (For example: "Event planned to [insert purpose]")

[City], [State]—[Your first sentence should be a power-packed one-liner that will grab the reader's attention and state the event type. Then go into the event's name, whom the event is for (whole community, children, youth, senior citizens, and so on), time, date, and place of the event.]

Unfortunately, PR is not always feel-good news stories, great content, and well-written press releases. PR also involves having a plan for when things go wrong. It is strategizing how to represent your brand. It is choosing how to communicate in the middle of a crisis that can make or break your brand. (More information on crisis communication is available in chapter 8).

PR and marketing could be perceived as serving the same purpose. However, the end goals are quite different: PR is used to establish and build trust within the community, whereas marketing is the process of getting people to buy into the vision. People have to know they can trust your church with their hurt, their brokenness, and their spiritual journeys (PR) before they ever decide to invest their time, energy, and money in your church and the work you are doing (marketing).

---

[3] Parts of this example press release were inspired by the Peninsula-Delaware Conference of the United Methodist Church, pen-del.org: "Sample Church Press Release Outline," Peninsula-Delaware Conference of the United Methodist Church, accessed March 28, 2021, https://www.pen-del.org/files/content/sample+pendel+church+press+release+outline.docx.

Chapter 8

Crisis Communication

Oh no. Someone in leadership said something that they should not have. Maybe the lead pastor made a culturally insensitive statement. A graphic was posted that does not reflect the church's mission, and hundreds of people saw it before it was removed. Someone on staff is suddenly facing criminal charges. Church property has been damaged. These moments are not when a crisis communication plan should be created. You do not have time to plan in a crisis. Churches are made up of imperfect people trying to bring heaven to earth. People make mistakes; they say things they should not and do things without thinking.

Unexpected situations pop up, and having a crisis communication plan ahead of time will help you navigate those situations with a clear road map during an unclear time. These plans provide guidance for what to do during the initial problem, how to communicate with the public, and how to prevent the issue from happening in the future.

How to Write a Crisis Communication Plan

First, identify the goal of this plan. An example of a goal statement could be, "The goal of this plan is to create an approach to correct internal views of the church's reputation if the lead pastor says something culturally insensitive that is not in alignment with the church's mission statement." Whatever goal is set, every aspect of the plan must funnel through this checkpoint. If it does not, adjust the strategy to cooperate or get rid of it. If a church uses a crisis communication plan, it is likely in a position where there is minimal room for error in response.

Second, determine whom this affects and who is offended. There could be multiple audiences, but some examples might include the congregation, the staff, the community, donors and stakeholders, the leadership board or elders, social media followers, and the general public. Similar to an advertising campaign, format your message to address these individual groups.

Next, create a diagram about who needs to know what. Prioritize internal stakeholders—your church members and employees. Big crises often switch on fear and panic for employees and members, so value your internal team and communicate openly with them. In the absence of information people will always make negative assumptions about the organization or institution. Have a plan for how to communicate emergencies to your teams. Most likely, it would be important that your lead pastor and leadership board know first, along with your communication team.

Then, add in different teams as needed, based on the category of crisis. For example, if the incident is in student ministry, it would be vital to include the students' staff in that conversation. Externally, the person who has the most information might not be the best person to be on the front lines giving information. In a corporate setting, the team who reports on the crisis is always the PR pro on the team. In a church setting, a PR professional on staff is most likely a dream rather than a reality. It is essential to designate a person for communication with the public or media. This person does not always need to be the main preaching pastor; in fact, this position might be better served by a discipleship pastor or executive pastor. Placing someone who cracks under pressure in front of a crowd to discuss uncomfortable topics will not benefit the plan. Choose a spokesperson who represents the church well and has a demeanor that fits the tone you want to portray. This person needs to be, as much as possible, the embodiment of the mission of the church.

Decide who should answer to the media and who can make those phone calls and be composed to respond appropriately. Find those people on the team and train them. In these moments, the last thing you need is for someone untrained to handle a crisis commentary and make it worse.

Create a fact sheet, scenario examples, and possible questions with their respective answers. A fact sheet is what you know to be real about the scenario, and it will help clear some confusion once the rumors about what happened begin. Whether it is a big or small crisis, people will hear X from a friend that turned into Y, and with the information they heard from their grandma, it turns into Z that they post about on social media. Write down what you know to be true. Scenario examples are when you think through every possible situation that could happen in this crisis. Think through the response strategy and start to build a communicative response ahead of time. These are preemptive measures, so it will most likely look like a skeleton outline, but it will give you direction when you need it most.

In your scenario examples, address potential risks as well. If all else fails and it all backfires, what are you left with? What does it look like to clean this up? Plan out the worst and best scenarios; this will allow your teams to be prepared and not caught off guard. For each of those scenarios, think through questions you might get and decide how you will respond as a team. Working through scenarios can be an excellent time to sit down with leadership and determine your church's tone in crisis. Are you respectful, empathetic, bold, understanding? Have this conversation before it is needed and have it again during the crisis. Tone in crisis will be determined by the crisis, but it is extremely important. If it is a sudden, shocking death, the tone will, of course, be shocked and saddened, but if it is a child molestation, the tone will still be shocked but also appalled. Preparing for the worst-case scenario is essential, especially when you're in charge of leading a team. The best way to do this is by thinking through questions and potential responses ahead of time to prepare your teams if something goes wrong. It can be hard to see what may happen down the line, but it's worth it because having contingencies ready means you're less likely to be caught off guard during an emergency. Once you've worked out all possible scenarios, determine how your church will respond as one unified voice with its tone set beforehand. Then, if everything does go well, at least now everyone knows what they should say!

A church leader should take three steps when taking responsibility for a mistake:

1. *Acknowledge*: Take responsibility for the action.
2. *Apologize*: Apologize and ease hurt people's emotions.
3. *Act*: Make changes to resolve the issue.

In some cases, not all of these need to be done at the exact same time. Steps 1 and 2 can be done together most often, but step 3 sometimes needs a time period of examination prior to making a statement.

Social media is virtually essential these days, but it is especially so in crisis communications. People can say anything, at any time, from any place, on any post. As a team, you have to be proactive in monitoring accounts and respectfully addressing concerns. Social media is there for everyone to see; there is no privacy, and what you say matters. Never delete comments to hide problems; respond according to the social media plan your team has created. If the strategy is to like every comment and message them privately, stick to it. If the process is to respond to every single comment in the same way and to look at a correlating post, stick to it. If the strategy is to customize each reply, stick to it. Inconsistency will give mixed signals. Set a plan in place, choose a tone, grab a cup of coffee, monitor those social platforms, and stick to the plan. Relate the response to the crisis's size. If replying on social media is not enough, consider having a dedicated banner on the church's website linking to an apology video. Social media has a lot of power in this situation; leverage it the best you can to be used for the mending process. These plans should be reviewed at least once a year. Make the changes necessary to fit where the church is in that season.

Have a crisis communication team that is diverse. If you are sitting around the table with people who look like you, have backgrounds similar to yours, and think like you, it will lead to unforeseen problems. This team should be a cross section of the church, including key laypeople, who work or volunteer in different ministries. From this group, it should start to become clear what possible crises may arise, how to best respond to a crisis at hand, and how to grow from a crisis after it has passed.

After a crisis, find and evaluate your new normal. The standard your church held precrisis no longer exists. Evaluate what your teams have learned, what has to change, and what those changes affect internally and externally. The worst thing that could happen is getting out of a crisis and not learning from mistakes, not implementing new policies, and watching it happen all over again. Work for the future of the church, not just the current climate.

Crises are never easy to navigate, and they are not a fun topic to discuss with leadership. However, having a set plan while not under stress will set you apart in crisis communication and prepare you for the future. Having this plan in place will help you navigate an uncertain time with more ease.

While this chapter is a good introduction to crisis communication, I suggest looking into more aspects, like a crisis budget, and considering other elements of possible crises. Communication will hinge on what the church has done proactively rather than reactively. Take the time, create the template, and prepare for the future.

Chapter 9

Leading a Team

The communication team oversees and protects the brand through various media channels, from the website, to social media, to print media. Many communication teams include smaller, individual teams such as marketing, creative, web, social media, and maybe even audio and video. You might be a one-man band. No matter the makeup of your team, you have to lead it.

Many churches see the communication team as a support staff role. However, your job is not just to market upcoming events but to be a partner in ministry when deciding how to best reach your people and communities with the gospel. You are the audience's voice in your church. You are the church member's voice. Some will say that if you are a communication director you do not wield any positional authority, and that might be true at some churches, but what you do have and will always have is relational authority. You have to fight to protect your audience from varying messages and to protect the church's brand. Ultimately, you are fighting to protect the mission. While a communication director may not be an authority, the communication director's voice is just as powerful as the senior pastor's because it is the senior pastor's voice coming through the communication channels. The communication director needs to be qualified, competent, and have a say at the executive table because of the influence they exercise. There will always be a lot of noise trying to reach your church's ears, but you are the guardian of their attention span. Wield this power carefully.

Many roles can be hired for a communication team:

- Graphic designer
- Creative director
- Project manager
- Video producer/director
- Writer/editor
- Web designer/developer/administrator
- Social media manager
- Print director[1]

Each role is important, and when you are building a communication staff it is important to weigh which roles you can and cannot do well yourself. Then consider which you can outsource online, if at all possible. For example, today there are many church graphic design companies that will do unlimited church graphics for a nominal monthly fee. These graphics could include sermon graphics, bulletins, or connection cards.

Most people do not and will not understand what you do, and even fewer will understand how you make their jobs better. Spend more time communicating with and educating your coworkers than anything else. Ask questions about their roles and their goals so you are better equipped to serve them. Realize that you have one of the most challenging roles on a church staff (because every department wants their thing communicated). Focus on building, empowering, and developing a world-class team around you.

To lead your team well, you need buy-in from your senior pastor. Once you have their confidence and a crystal-clear understanding of their vision, you can set strategy and priorities and welcome others to the team. By way of contrast, each ministry has its own vision and priorities, and you can get caught in the middle by reacting instead of leading as they compete against one another for bandwidth. Do not make this mistake. Instead, establish early on what the expectations

---

[1] For more information on how to incorporate traditional and print media into your communication strategy, see appendix G.

are for your role from your supervisors, then reconcile those with your own expectations of your work. Your job is to help connect the vision of the ministry to the overall vision or mission of the church. The role of communication director must encourage all to be part of the one story of the church. Essentially, you are the chief storyteller at the church.

Finally, if you have a team and you are not just a team of one, consider yourself blessed. In many churches around the world the pastor is doing all these roles on top of their already chaotic job. If you have a team, be grateful for them. Support them. Educate them. Spend time with them. Do not be a bottleneck; be an energizer. Give compassion and grace when necessary. Read and study management. Continue learning about how to lead a team well. No one was born a manager. Management is a skill that is acquired after years of experience and education.

Leading a team can be overwhelming. It is important to remember that you can say no to certain things that do not fall within the set expectations for your job. Create boundaries for yourself and for your team to thrive and survive. You'll have to explain the *why* over and over to people with each new request and project. But remember, it is your job to protect your church's brand and the audience. Honor people as best you can, and give lots of grace. This is where the church as an organization can follow the golden rule and be an example to the other ministries inside the church.

Leading When You Are Not in Charge

Leadership can come in many forms. A title on a desk plate is not what defines a leadership mentality. Just because you do not have the term *director* or *manager* in your title does not mean you cannot have a leadership mindset. Leadership is within the individual, not the title. You can lead even when you are not the boss.

Begin leading right where you are. Every person on a team is responsible for something. No matter how big or small, everyone is accountable for something. Steward what you have well. Even if it is just making sure something is posted at precisely the right time, you post that, and you post it right on the dot! You do not do a job for applause or admiration, but leadership notices excellence when you steward well. In addition to working toward excellence in your responsibilities, be a leader who thinks critically. You do not have to be the boss to look at procedures and concepts and make them better. Ask questions, be aware of every aspect of a project, and connect the answers to solutions to move the job forward. However, there is a difference between critical thinking and being critical. Come to the table with solutions, not just judgments. Be a critical thinker and a problem solver. Whether you are communicating solutions or ideas, communicate clearly. You cannot expect people to know your thoughts, worries, concerns, or anything else if you do not share. Drop passive-aggressiveness, pick up assertive tendencies, and say what you mean. Everyone on a team has a voice; use yours to communicate care for the project and care for your teammates.

Lead where you are as a team player. Leaders are there to serve a team and drive a project or department forward. You do not need a specific job title to be a team player. Engage other people on your team, help your teammates when they need it, and listen to their ideas. Each teammate holds a lot of influence in the room, whether you are the new intern or the boss. The attitude a team member brings to the table can completely shift the entire team; we have all felt it. Make sure you lead with a progressive perspective that puts forth a can-do attitude. Always come to the table asking how you can add value to this team and this idea. Do not sit back just because you do not have an official title. Lead with your mindset, and lead with your influence. The greatest asset you have is how you choose to think; choose wisely.

Choose a positive and diligent attitude. Go into the office every day knowing that your boss and your team have chosen to do things a certain way, and trust that they know what they are doing. Put 110 percent of your effort into making it the best it can be. That is how you influence, that is how you show up for your team, and that is how you lead when you are not the boss.

Finally, be a great leader to yourself. Take the initiative, and be ambitious about your goals. Set clear goals for yourself so they are attainable. Lead yourself well in addition to allowing your boss to lead you. The concept of "you cannot keep filling people up if you are not being poured into" applies here. Your leaders are in their positions for a reason. Learn from them, value their roles, respect their positions. You show respect to something while working to be like it. You are responsible for being your own motivator. Take calculated risks—it can be nerve-wracking, but be scared and do it anyway. Charge ahead with zeal, and accomplish everything you set out to accomplish. Make a project the best it can be, strive for excellence, be creative, be innovative, and be forward-thinking. Be bold in your work ethic and leadership. Boldness has remarkable potential if you just take the first step. You are going to fail along the way, but what's more important than the failure itself is how you move forward. Proudly learn from your mistakes, and reevaluate how you move forward. Great leaders have made mistakes, and that will include you. How you pick yourself back up says more about your leadership than the error itself.

Remember, becoming a leader does not just happen overnight. It takes time and intentionality to become great at something. Take it upon yourself to wake up every day and choose to better yourself for those around you and yourself.

Chapter 10

Project Management and Handling Communications Requests

Hopefully, you have never been here, but the reality is, most church communicators have experienced the dreaded Monday morning when the pastor or ministry leader comes into their work area demanding an explanation as to why their promotion did not make the cut for the service. The worst part is when the only answer you have is some version of "I forgot." It is easy to become overwhelmed, stressed out, and forgetful in a position that requires working with so many different ministries and advertising so many events to various audiences. This is where a communications calendar comes in handy. A church communications calendar is a planning tool to help your church become proactive instead of reactive. It is where you go to process requests, set marketing plans, and plan your month and your year.

How to Plan a Communications Calendar

First, invest in a good-quality fifty-two-week calendar (maybe a dry-erase one; see churchcommunications.com/calendar). Mount it somewhere you can see it. Next, look at your church calendar and the recurring yearly events, such as Easter, Christmas, vacation Bible school, or youth conference. Plan those first. Think about how long you need to promote each event, and put it on the calendar. You'll be surprised about how many weeks that takes up.

Ideally, after you determine your major events, you will set up your communications calendar for ninety days in advance. Now, you might be reading this, thinking, "There is no way I can do ninety days. I barely know what's going on in two weeks!" That is okay! If ninety days is too much to tackle at one time, start small. Try thirty days. Plan out four weeks' worth of communication, including video announcements, promotional social posts (and what social platforms to use), bulletin or magazine ads, banners, Sunday platform announcements, and so on. Try to work up slowly to planning communication strategies ninety days in advance of events.

Project Management

Face it—all great ideas have the opportunity to fall flat without a plan to prioritize projects, assignments, due dates, and tasks. It happens so often. You have an excellent idea for a family movie night or a worship night, or you launch a new ministry, and it falls through because someone, somewhere, at some point did not do what they were supposed to do. Disorganization is why many great ideas go stale and just sit in the virtual filing cabinet collecting dust. Whether you have a large or small church, project management and organization are vital to any organization moving projects forward.

Every ministry within your organization or church should implement project management. Collectively, you have to stay organized, and your ministries have to be fluid with one another. If you are all moving in different directions, project management allows you to all get on the same track and move forward as a team. To accomplish this, organize each ministry individually and collectively as a whole church. The organization allows your ministry teams to succeed as a cohesive unit, but it also allows you to all come together seamlessly.

Think about it like any sport, such as basketball. Each NBA team functions as its own unit: the Chicago Bulls operate very differently than the Miami Heat. They have different players and coaches, they practice various drills, they have different playbooks, and they serve as their specialized unit within the NBA organization. However, when they play a game with another team, they play under the same rules and guidelines. Every ministry should have its own playbook that operates within the church's parameters as a whole. Your ministries' playbooks should include things like budgeting, calendaring, time management tools, and appropriately assigning tasks that fit the skill sets of particular staff or volunteers. For example, would the Chicago Bulls ever put Michael Jordan in a point guard position meant for shorter teammates when Michael is six foot six and excels at being a shooting guard? No. So why put your staff and volunteers in a position they will not excel in when you have other prime opportunities open for them? Also set clear expectations to ensure your teams can meet them. These tips prioritize time spent on projects and help each ministry efficiently and effectively stay on task.

Project management can look different based on the size of the church. Larger churches may want to funnel all aspects of ministry through the communications department to ensure no overlap or miscommunication between ministries takes place. In comparison, smaller churches may benefit from something keeping them on task and a system that onboards new staff and volunteers. Communication on a platform that ensures everyone has access to information during a project or change is essential. Communication is a collaborative effort that can improve your church's effectiveness, accountability, strategy, and goals.

To evaluate what would be the most effective project management style for your church, take note of the entire scope and sequence of needs. What is it your team keeps letting slip through the cracks? What are you not accomplishing consistently that needs to change? What do you need? This is a good time to talk to your ministry leaders and really listen to what they have to say about what is falling short in and out of their department. Some of this may be good for the crisis communication team to be aware of too. Everyone has blind spots in their ministry, so having others weigh in confidentially can be helpful to gauge where your teams are excelling and where things could be improved. Based on these responses, find a free or paid application that works best for your needs. These different systems are not one size fits all—look around at what is available, and find what suits your team and needs best. Regardless of what system you choose, your communication team should have a project management system to keep all requests organized.

For example, the church is having a students' worship night. The students team put in a request for social media graphics and advertisements. Your worship team also put in a request. These requests are for the same event, so they need the same branding. Having a project management system for your communications team allows you to recognize the similarity and save time and resources that would have been spent making different graphics for two different departments that are ultimately for the same event. Another example is a request made for a project, but three weeks later the entire scope of the project takes a complete 180-degree turn. Using a project management system can ensure that everyone is alerted and aware of the changes and can respond accordingly so everyone is on the same page. These systems promote accountability and transparency throughout projects.

It might be challenging to get everyone to be in a state where they completely understand why these systems are necessary. It might seem like you are over their shoulder, checking in on them often. But promote the benefits of these systems to your teams and encourage them to buy into the concept. Lead by example; if you are excited about it, the team will be excited about it. Have a project manager keep track of all expectations, deadlines, and tasks. This person will guide teams to stay on track and complete projects by their assigned deadlines. Every member of the team should be informed, from interns to lead pastors.

There are many resources, tools, and strategies to implement project management. Check out some of the existing project management methods, such as Waterfall, Scrum, Agile, and Kanban.[1] The Waterfall method is based on the requirement that in a project, each task must be completed sequentially before moving on to the next.[2] This methodology does not permit regression to earlier phases of the process, so if something changes, the entire project must be restarted. For example, when you bake a cake, you cannot frost the batter. The cake making requires a certain flow of tasks in order to be completed. If you change the batter flavor at the last second, you cannot just combine the completed cake with a new flavor; you have to fully restart.

Waterfalls are less flexible than their counterpart, the Agile methodology. The Agile method is adaptive and breaks projects down into subsections.[3] Agile methods offer a lot of flexibility and are often a welcome change. Kanban methodology is a subset of Agile methodology. Kanban's goal is to coordinate and level the workload of team members.

---

[1] Lucid Content Team, "Agile vs. Waterfall vs. Kanban vs. Scrum," *Lucidchart Blog*, October 9, 2019, https://www.lucidchart.com/blog/agile-vs-waterfall-vs-kanban-vs-scrum.

[2] Lucid Content Team.

[3] Lucid Content Team.

Kanban implements a board that is broken down into sections titled "work to be done," "work in progress," and "completed work."[4] As a team progresses through tasks, those tasks are moved along the board so the team can visualize where the project is currently. This method provides accountability and transparency of tasks among team members. Scrum methodology is all about efficiency and completing tasks as quickly as possible. This is a really great method for time crunches or when projects are dropped on a team with little notice. Scrum methodology is broken down into what are called sprints: these are two-week periods where teams complete projects that are highly organized and meticulously planned out prior to those two weeks.[5] At the beginning of each workday, the team holds a quick meeting to discuss problems, solutions, and progress. Some project management systems are Asana, Monday, Basecamp, and Workfront.

Success in project management can be a lot of work because an organization or church involves a lot of work. But it will keep your team on track, help you reach goals with more ease over time, and deliver results from different ministries that align with the church as an organized entity.

A church can follow this simple framework to keep things moving forward:

1. Create a project plan.
2. Identify the stakeholders (such as ministry leaders) and their needs.
3. Determine the goals of the project, how it will be evaluated, and who will be responsible for each step in the process.
4. Determine what resources are needed to complete this project.
5. Set timelines for completing tasks or milestones within a reasonable timeframe (e.g., weekly).
6. Establish deadlines for when work is due and when reports should be submitted to supervisors or other stakeholders.

Step One: Create a Project Plan

First, identify the purpose of the event or ministry the church is promoting. What problem does this event solve? Who is involved? Determine

---

[4] Lucid Content Team.
[5] Lucid Content Team.

what the church wants to achieve from the event itself. Second, decide who is the target audience for this event or ministry. Clearly define the target audience using segmentation. The church could create a persona, if necessary. Decide on a date and time for promotion. When is the event? How long will it last? Where is the event? Third, decide on a budget for promotion of the event or ministry. Does the event or ministry have a budget line for promotion? If it does not, can people volunteer their time to help promote it? Fourth, find out what kind of activities will be happening at the event or get a written description of the ministry. In this step, the church might also brainstorm the event's theme, food, agenda, and so on. Fifth, find out who are the stakeholders in this event and ministry. Are there people the communication team will need to run ideas by before committing to them? Who else might need to know about your project plan before it starts, and when should they know about it? Sixth, create a timeline for each task that needs to be completed and for completion of the project. Finally, develop an action plan to recruit volunteers and staff members to delegate tasks, as well as identify any potential obstacles that may arise during the event or ministry.

Step Two: Identify the Stakeholders and Their Needs

Make a list of everyone who has a stake in the project. List all the church leaders, the project manager, any contractors, volunteers, congregation members, ministry leaders, and even donors. Then go back through that list and define what they need from the communication team and from the communication director.

Step 3: Determine the Goals of the Project, How They Will Be Evaluated, and Who Will Be Responsible for Each Step in the Process

After you have created the project plan and defined the stakeholders and their needs, it is time to list how the goals of this project relate to the high-level goals of the church. Determine the goals of this event or ministry with the ministry leader implementing the project. Make sure that all goals are SMART goals. Determine what success looks like. After you have set up your goals, start assigning those goals to specific people. Ensure that both the communication team and the ministry team you are working with know the overall goal toward which they are working.

Step 4: Determine What Resources Are Needed to Complete This Project

Determine a list of resources that will be needed to make the project happen. Questions to consider include: What budget does the ministry have to work with? Does part of the budget come from our team or their team? Will facilities need to be managed? Write a list of everything physical that will need to be handled and be sure to assign those tasks.

Step 5: Set Timelines for Completing Tasks or Milestones Within a Reasonable Timeframe

First, define the task or milestone. Break down the tasks into groups of tasks or milestones, set deadlines with dates on these milestones, and determine what success will look like at each milestone. If the project is larger, split it into manageable pieces to guarantee everybody is on the same page. Keep the timeline in front of the communication director at all times; this is where a project management tool becomes helpful.

Many communication teams will create packages that already have set milestones with tasks, and then the ministry will choose a package. That package will have set deadlines and dates, and a timeline for how far ahead of the event the communication team needs to begin in order to be successful.

Step 6: Establish Deadlines for When Work Is Due and When Reports Should Be Submitted to Supervisors or Other Stakeholders

Set timelines for completing tasks or milestones within a reasonable timeframe. Before assigning tasks, check the team's workload to see if they can handle any additional work. Be careful not to load too much onto a team at one time. Also, this is a good time to establish whether the task doer needs to check with their supervisor before and after doing a task or if they should simply do the task without asking beforehand and reporting afterward. Each supervisor is different, but be careful not to start micromanaging the team.

Communication Requests

Many communication teams at churches live and die by their communications request system. A communication request system is simply a form that feeds into a project management system, as discussed previously. The system can be a blessing and a curse. It can be a blessing because you can keep track of the various tasks on your team's plate, but it can be a curse because many departments will feel they can request anything they want from your department. The communication request form can be as complex or as simple as you want. Some churches also choose to track their communication requests so departments and ministries know where their team is in the process. First, you have to figure out what exactly you are going to put on your form. You may have one form with a drop-down menu and many conditional form fields that require you to make decisions; then different form fields appear based on those decisions. Think about what best serves your church and your communication team. You might want multiple forms—one for video, one for marketing, one for media requests, and so on.

Additionally, you may want to consider how your team receives requests. Do you handle every request, or do you have a system by which people can receive support for their events and ministries? For example, many churches have tiers of support depending on the type of event or ministry and what that event or ministry can expect in marketing, video, communication, and media support. A tier one event would be an all-hands-on-deck event that involves every member of the church. Maybe it is a major community outreach event. That means this event automatically gets a flier, banner, website ad, social media posts, and so on. If it is a tier two event that involves one or two ministries of the church, many people are involved but not the entire church. Perhaps it is VBS. Many parents and children attend VBS, but it is not for the entire church, so the event would get a flier, banner, website ad, and social media posts, but it would require fewer things than a major tier one event.

You might also consider how far out someone can submit a request. Can they submit a request that is due today, or does it have to be two weeks out? It's up to you.

There are many online form builders available, including the following:

- Wufoo.com
- Jotform.com
- Gravity Forms Plugin for WordPress

On the following page is an example of a communications request form done in Microsoft Word.

Communication Request Form Example[6]

Insert your logo here

Communication Request Form

Please complete this form and return it to the Church Administrative Assistant.

The Communication Team is here to help you get the word out about your ministry event and or communication needs! We strive to reflect the heart of your event while maintaining the best practices to ensure effectiveness, clarity, and consistency. Since there is a limited amount of time, energy and space that can be given to communications at YOUR CHURCH NAME, we sometimes have to make difficult decisions about what things will be promoted in which capacities. Any communication decisions are made based on the church's mission and core values and the purpose, target audience, timeframe and detail of the requested event.

*Please note that until your request is **submitted in its entirety** (dates, contact information, written material, etc.) we cannot lock in a deadline. We need to have **all** information before we can guarantee a completion date. **Even if you do your own design, it needs to have Pastoral approval before being used. Finalization of communications will be at the discretion of Pastor and the Communication Team.**

COMMUNICATION TIMELINE		
	Date	**Required Timeframe**
Event Date:		Date of Actual Event
Initial Run Date:		Usually 4 weeks prior to Event Date
Graphics Request Deadline:		2 weeks prior to the *Run Date (at least)*
Video/Print Request Deadline:		4 Weeks prior to *Run Date (at least)*

EVENT DETAILS					
Event Name:		**Event Date(s):**			
Location of Event:		**Cost:**			
Ministry:		**Target Audience:**			
Event Leader:		**Leader Email:**			
Leader Phone:		**Start Time:** (AM/PM)		**End Time:**	(AM/PM)
Full Written Description of Event and Design Ideas (if any): *Use Separate Paper If needed					

Page 1 of 2

---

[6] "Communication Request Form" provided by Ellen Graeber Knight via email, March 8, 2021.

Communication Types Requested:

Item	Timeframe	Budget Allotted	Design Approved	Assigned
General Media				
❑ Bulletin/YouVersion ❑ Facebook Announcement ❑ Facebook Event ❑ PowerPoint Slide Template	• *At least TWO weeks* in advance of *Run Date* in order to be considered.	N/A		
Video				
❑ Testimony ❑ Announcement ❑ Promo Video (Pastoral Use Only)	• *At least FOUR weeks* in advance of *Run Date* in order to be considered. • Please give your main idea in as much detail as possible on a separate page.	N/A		
In-House Printing				
❑ Foyer Poster ❑ Registration Form ❑ Flyers ❑ Postcards/Invitations	• *At least FOUR weeks* in advance of *Run Date* in order to be considered.			
Professional Printing				
❑ Banners/Signs ❑ Business Cards ❑ Postcards ❑ Mugs/Pens/Other	• *At least FOUR-SIX weeks* in advance of *Run Date* in order to be considered.			

What You Can Expect from the Communications Team

- Within 2 Business days of receiving the request, initial follow-up with deadline commitment and request for any further information.
- The Communication Team will use materials that are free from copyright infringement to the best of their ability and will avoid using images/video/fonts/vectors/music that will violate copyrights and or require licensures.
- Publishing of the communication will take place at regular intervals determined by the Communication Team for each media type. The event leaders can and should invite people verbally and via social media as much as possible to also promote the event. For Facebook Announcements and Events, it's very important to have your entire team RSVP, Post, Share, Invite, Like and Comment on all materials posted.
- Any printed materials will have a draft/approval process beginning at least one week out from run date.
- You will be notified via email when printed materials are available for pick-up.
- If you need access to any digital files they will be made available via Drop Box and/or Email, or USB Drive.

OFFICE USE ONLY			
Date Request Received:		Date Approved:	
Assigned To:		Date Assigned:	

Chapter 11

First Ninety Days

What would your first twelve weeks contain if you were getting started at a church doing church communication? The first ninety days of a church communications position can be daunting. How do I get started? What should I do? This chapter will provide a practical guide for church communications directors to help them navigate the first ninety days in their new role. While this is a week-by-week guide, these weeks don't have to go in any particular order, and you may find it's more of a month-by-month guide instead. The most important thing is not to burn out; this is a marathon, not a race. Take your time.

Week 1: Communication Audit & Survey

The first activity I would do when I arrive at church is to better understand the lay of the land, both internally and externally. Understanding your church can be done in two ways—first through a marketing audit and then through a survey.

A communication audit includes reviewing the church's website, social media presence, and print and other offline materials, and interviewing key stakeholders. It should be led by someone who can objectively look at those areas and provide recommendations for improving them.

Internal stakeholder interviews should include the leadership team and any departments that regularly interact with website visitors, participants in social media, and people who receive church communications (if those areas exist). If you don't have a business or marketing background, I encourage you to recruit someone from your church to help you in this area. Additionally, you can hire an outside firm to complete this marketing audit. Once the communication audit is complete, it will be helpful to set up a time with your leadership team or board to review it and discuss recommendations for improvement.

After the communication audit has been completed, it's time for the survey. There is an example of a congregation survey in Appendix C. It would be helpful also to survey the community for opinions about your church; this external survey can be done anecdotally or through a focus group.

Week 2: Gather Current Marketing Collateral

Next, we need to gather all the current marketing collateral. What is your church's brand? Where is the logo? Are the assets all available for use? What are the currently approved color palettes for print, web, and social media?

Based on what you found through your audit and survey, you'll be able to compile this marketing collateral. It's key to make sure all your materials match both internally across marketing channels and externally with each other. Having matching marketing collateral is particularly important if you have a formal brand identity system in place.

Figure out where all the files are and where all the logins are, and then file them away correctly if they weren't previously. If you don't know the file locations, ask someone in IT or your church administrator.

You'll want to start with all printed materials currently in use and compile them into a single binder or folder for easy access. Then review all digital assets (including your website) and pull graphics/ images to be used in social media posts. It's helpful to have a place for all your current marketing assets so that when you recreate print, website, and social media materials, the files will be instantly available.

Weeks 3–4: Start Work on Your New Marketing Strategy

In chapter 1, we go into detail about how to create a marketing strategy. Now is the time to get to work. Take a couple of weeks to dive into mission and vision. Figure out your church's values. Find time to get internal stakeholders and leadership on board in this process. Then create customer personas and work on your marketing strategy.

I highly recommend doing this process in the order it is laid out in chapter 1 so that you can refine your church's mission, vision, values, and brand identity before actually creating marketing materials for them. The marketing strategy plan will save you time in the long run.

In week 4, take time for a SWOT analysis. The SWOT analysis is a crucial element of your marketing strategy since it will help you determine what you're already great at and what areas need improvement. After you've completed your SWOT analysis, you'll be able to create a marketing plan.

Now that you've got the foundation in place (mission, vision, values), it's time to create a new marketing plan or edit your old one. You'll need to detail your goals, target audiences (customer personas), marketing mix, and how you plan to track success.

Don't be afraid to get creative with your new strategy. Even if it's a small church, your approach can still be unique and compelling. You might even consider taking a marketing class and allowing yourself to be inspired by other businesses, industries, or organizations.

Your marketing plan should include goals and objectives for the next one to two years. In addition, it must consist of a documented strategy for how you will achieve these goals and objectives. You can't expect results without a strategic plan to work toward them.

You should have a marketing plan for digital as well as print and physical assets. Digital channels are constantly changing, so having a documented strategy that can be repeatedly executed is key to ensuring you're not just chasing fads online.

Week 5: Launch Your Marketing Strategy

Now that you have a marketing strategy, it's time to launch it! First, do a sermon series on your new mission and vision. The new mission, vision, and values should be reiterated in your sermon series. Next, suppose you're creating videos or podcasts to communicate these topics. In that case, you'll edit the video every time it's played so that the mission statement is playing while people are seeing images of what it looks like in practice by creating a video bumper for the series.

Next, review your church's values with your congregation. Finally, create marketing collateral around these recent statements for your church body. You can also launch social media posts and ad campaigns around these topics.

If you've created print materials for this launch, schedule a time to send these items out. Also, update your website with the new mission and vision statements. If you don't have a website or it is outdated, then it's time to set aside some funds and invest in creating a new one to contain all your unique branding elements.

You'll also want to implement your social media strategy. Post on every platform consistently and strategically so that you build relationships with seekers. Don't just post because you can. Post with a purpose to engage with your target audiences and to help them take the next step in faith formation.

Week 6: Understand Your Current Projects and Tasks

Now that you've launched your marketing strategy, it's essential to understand what is already in the works (projects) and what needs to be done next (tasks). Knowing this information will help you with prioritizing and planning.

If there are any projects currently in the works, assess their success factors and see if they were achieved. If they were, that's fantastic! If not, then it's time to reevaluate if you should continue with them or scrap them altogether.

Additionally, you'll want to prioritize all the tasks that need to be done. This prioritization process will take some time, so don't expect to have it all figured out right away. What needs to be done next is up to you.

Evaluate current projects by asking the following questions:

- Does my new mission and vision reflect the church's core values?
- Are there any gaps between the new mission and vision versus the church's current practices?

- Do I know my target audiences (customer personas) better than I did before?
- Did my marketing plan adequately cover each marketing channel (digital, print, physical)?
- Was my social media strategy effective in engaging people?

You're almost there! Hopefully, you've got an understanding of your current projects and tasks prioritized. This is where a marketing plan with goals and objectives will come in handy to determine what steps to take next toward achieving your vision.

If you don't have a strategy or didn't write any goals and objectives, it's time to go back and start there. A large part of your new marketing plan reflects your current projects and tasks for the next one to two years. You can't just focus on one project or task unless it ties in with your vision statement.

Week 7: Plan Your Church Comm Calendar

In week seven, you should begin to develop your plan for how church communication efforts will unfold. Part of this is creating a calendar with all your marketing and communication efforts and when they should occur.

You'll want to develop a plan for the calendar at least six months in advance (for preaching, missions, worship services). With social media, you can be more fluid in how often you post with different types of content on each platform. However, it's still a good idea to have a calendar for this as well.

Plan out your digital and print formats along with the frequency with which you'll need them by asking yourself these questions:

- What kinds of things will I say on my website?
- When will I be sending out updates via email?
- How often will I share content from social media platforms?
- What kind of content will I be sharing (relevant articles, sermons, images)?
- Will this be easy for me to maintain on my own, or should I plan to hire someone else to help with this?

Your Church Comm Calendar can help guide you in the future and help keep your planning proactive rather than reactive.

Weeks 8–9: Begin Work on an Advertising Campaign

The next few weeks are for beginning your advertising campaign. First, create an ad that will compel people to come to your church. And don't just choose an advertisement because you think it would look cool, but rather spend time considering what message you're trying to communicate and how you want people to feel about taking the next step in faith formation with your church.

Your church should have a standard ad that you'll see on all advertising platforms. For example, if your church has a new website design, it's time to brand your ads with the new look and feel of the website. And don't forget about using the same image across all social media channels as well. Choosing your ad collateral is essential. Be wise when selecting pictures and messaging to convey who your church is to your community.

Choosing your ad platforms is equally important. Each ad platform can reach different people. Facebook and Google ads are typical mainstream ads and easy to get started with, but you might consider print ads too in your local area. We usually suggest churches do not spend more than $500 initially, so it's essential to set goals and achieve them.

Can you accomplish your goals with Facebook ads? Maybe, but what about Google ads? Consider what you're trying to achieve in each ad campaign before choosing one or the other. Think about how many people in your community use that platform and if it will even be helpful to you.

Week 10: Launch Campaign

You're ready to start spending money on your advertising campaign at this point. You've created and planned your ads, and you've chosen the platforms to use. Now, push that "go" button and launch!

Remember, there's no such thing as a perfect campaign, so don't put too much pressure on yourself up front. It's essential to just get started. Also, it will help if you have already mapped out your goals for this campaign, so it will be easier to measure the success of your ads once they are live.

Week 11: Understand Your Metrics

After the first two weeks, spend some time evaluating various aspects of what's working in your marketing plan. For example, are your mission and vision resonating? Do the values make sense? Do they need to be changed? Does the SWOT analysis need to be updated?

Next, spend some time considering what's working in your advertising campaign. Using the goals you established in your marketing plan, set up key performance indicators along the way so you know you're meeting those goals. What kind of open and click-through rates are you seeing on your ads? Are they even reaching people, or does it seem like all the impressions are going to bots or uninterested parties?

Make sure to take the time to understand what's working and what isn't. You'll be surprised at how much you learn about yourself, your church, your community, and your marketing plan.

Week 12: Evaluate What You've Done and Readjust

It's time to step back and think through the previous eleven weeks. What worked? What didn't work? Could you have done something differently? Asking yourself these questions is essential to refining your marketing plan for future success.

Think about some of the specific challenges you've faced with this first ad campaign. Did you make any wrong assumptions? What could you do differently in the future to improve your next ad campaign?

This final week is also an excellent time to think about your budget and whether or not it's working. For example, did you spend too much money on Facebook ads, and now you're trying to recover from that by spending more money on print ads in your local paper? Do you need to go back and adjust your goals since you didn't reach them the first time around?

All of these questions are essential to understanding what was successful in this campaign. From there, you'll have a better idea of what needs to be changed going forward.

You are done! Congratulations on making it through your first ninety days as a church communicator.

Chapter 12

What to Do Now

Church communication, especially where it concerns technology and social media, is a whole new realm of possibilities. Just twenty years ago, this job did not exist; the main communicator was the pastor. But now there are so many new media that it sometimes takes a team to manage all of it.

All of the new media that churches have access to has opened new doors to share the gospel in ways we only dreamed about even just a decade ago. The medium might have changed, but the message of the gospel has not. The message of hope and salvation found in Jesus Christ is more important than ever in these ever-changing times. We can thank God that while these media change, he has not.

Communication is often a never-ending and thankless job. I would not prepare you well if I did not say it can be overwhelming and difficult. You might experience lots of opposition to new means of communication, but it is important to look past the opposition and look to Jesus and his example. Essentially, we are storytellers on a mission. That mission has looked different throughout history, but the goal has remained the same: to spread the gospel of Jesus to the ends of the earth using whatever means or media necessary.

Remember, when in doubt ask yourself: Whom am I trying to reach? What do they do? Where are they from? Become like Paul, a man who became all things to all people (1 Cor 9:22). Remembering who your target audience is will help inform all your marketing and communication decisions moving forward.

Communication is more than a service department for the church. Communication is a ministry of the church itself. Communicating well is one of the best gifts a church can give not only its congregation and ministries, but also its community. When you communicate clearly, everyone wins.

My prayer for you, church communicator, is that even when you are not seen, you still realize your value. That when there is chaos in crisis, God is clear, and words come easily. I pray you find a place where your ministry is respected, and you grow. And finally, I pray you communicate the gospel clearly . . . until the whole world hears.

Appendix A: How to Create a Persona

The first step to creating a persona is research about your congregation, who is in your community, what the community wants, and where the community is going. A persona includes gender, age, former denomination or religious affiliation, any felt needs, income level, and education level.

Personas should be representative of your church body. Consequently, all church leaders must agree on what their personas are. Creating personas is a part of market research, and how you go about doing it is important. There are many sources for market research. Here are a few to get you started:

- Use whatever information you already have on hand. You might have ideas about your church members based on research done in the past or by simply knowing your members.
- Make assumptions. If you have been working at a church for a while, you may have enough knowledge to make relatively accurate assumptions about your church members.

- Use web analytics. People often underestimate the value of cold, hard data from your church's website. Do not overlook this information.
- Conduct interviews with church members. Nothing beats talking to a real person.
- Create focus groups in your church and in your community.
- Complete surveys.

Of course, you do not want to know just about your church members; you also want to know about the people you are trying to reach. Take time to do some surveys with your community concerning who they are and your church's identity within the community. Consider forming a focus group with people who do not attend your church, and ask them questions about what they would like to see in a church and the community—you might be surprised.

The second step is to segment your audience or congregation. Your church audience can usually be subdivided into three rings of people:[1]

- Those who already know of and attend your church
- Those who are seeking a new church due to relocation or those who are merely looking for something different
- Those who are seeking something that your church offers— for example, help with a "felt need" that can be provided by one of your ministries. You can consider these people to be un-churched—often called *seekers*.

Here are some questions you can ask while developing these personas:

- Are they similar to or different from your typical church member? Different? How?
- Are they married or single? Female or male? What is their income level? Education level?
- What goals are they accomplishing in their spiritual lives by attending church?
- What challenges are they facing in their spiritual lives?
- What can we do to help them achieve their goals and overcome their challenges?

---

[1] "MII University," Media Impact International, accessed September 2, 2021, https://www.mii.global.

- After you have answered these questions, give that person a name. Refer to him or her often. How can you reach the "Jasons" and "Megans" of your community?

Appendix B: PESO's Place in the Church

Companies and churches have the same need in advertising: finding the right mixture of platforms, messages, and ways to get information out to their publics effectively. The PESO model includes four different types of media: paid, earned, shared, and owned. Using a variation of integrated aspects of the PESO model is a highly efficient way for an organization to release information or advertising pieces. This appendix will explain each medium in the PESO model, the benefits, and how to use the PESO model at your church.[1]

Paid Media

Anything related to advertising, which is traditionally paid for by a brand, falls under the term *paid media*. Paid tactics are the standard when you think of corporate advertising, and they have a handy place in church advertising. Some paid media examples are publications,

[1] Gini Dietrich, "What Is the PESO Model? Integration of the Four Media Types," Spin Sucks, March 5, 2020, https://spinsucks.com/what-is-the-peso-model.

local radio stations, online ad placements (e.g., Instagram, Facebook, YouTube, Google), SEO, sponsorships, and others. The church is paying for the ad space or a time slot for the content for which they are creating a campaign. They are paying those platforms to drive traffic back to their landing page, website, or even the church's building on Sunday. Therefore, it needs to be strategically planned in advance with clear goals in mind. Do not throw money away on something without a clear purpose other than to see if it works. Online platforms typically have a clear and detailed breakdown of audiences, so place ads according to your audience and where they are most active. Typically, generating new traffic to your landing pages is immediate. Ensure that the pages where these paid ads are sending people have tactics to keep them there and grab their attention, and have a strategy in place to accomplish the set goal.

With paid media (unlike other media) the organization has total control: the organization can initiate and stop ads whenever they wish or cancel or restart them. Most websites and social media platforms have measuring tools built in. A communication director can track where people are coming from and determine which ads are working and which ones to stop. Platforms such as Ad Espresso, Hootsuite Ads, Facebook Ads Manager, and Google AdWords allow users to create a more detailed and comprehensive report on their advertising.

One problem with paid media is that there is often no lasting connection between the church and the reached audience after the ad run is completed. If the church has a limited budget, it is not a sustainable method to create connections. Additionally, there will be competition when leveraging paid media, so design the content accordingly.

In the church, big dates are days such as Easter, Christmas, and worship nights, as well as VBS and other special events. Therefore, it makes sense to advertise these. It is essential to get the word out about the events that most churches have, but advertising should also set the church apart. Grab viewers' attention despite them seeing other advertisements for the same thing at another location. In a world of media distraction, it cannot be stressed enough how important it is to be creative and think outside the box. How can an ad be created that will "stop the scroll" on social media? What kind of billboard ad will make someone wonder? What ad creative and copy needs to be created to communicate an important event in a newspaper ad? Paid media can help churches expand outside their circle of influence and reach people who are far from Christ.

Earned Media

Earned media is the basis of media relations; getting your message out must be earned by sending out information to different outlets and journalists. Your message must be convincing enough for a journalist to think it is of high value to their audience. Programs like Muck Rack or Cision have compiled data systems of journalists, bloggers, news anchors, independent journalists, radio hosts, and others across the country with their beats (their specialty topics they cover), contact information, and work samples. You have to pay for these media lists. However, you can do it the old-fashioned way and put pen to paper, dig online, and create your own media contact lists.

Before sending content out to journalists, walk through these steps: clearly define the goal of the content you are sending, define your audience and their preference of media and how they receive it, and have ways to measure effectiveness.

Reviews are another means of earned media. An example would be product reviews by people who have experienced what you have to offer. Reviews sway opinion rather quickly because they speak about the experience of a consumer who has the same intentions. For example, when I consider buying something on Amazon and it has terrible reviews, I move on. (Products are similar to experiences, except that a church experience has a lot more that goes into it than a simple one-time purchase.) With reviews, you have the power to turn regular people into advocates for a company, product, or, in your case, the church. A downside of earned media is that you do not have control over the response. You cannot control bad reactions, and deleting them does not look good for your church's reputation either. However, you do have the opportunity to mend relationships. If you get a bad review, that is your chance to listen and reply appropriately.

Earned media is free, works well to spread awareness of who your church is, and is a big part of media relations and public relations efforts. Earned media is used to measure public opinion and build awareness of your church through other people's good ideas of what you do. Measuring engagement and buzz around your church is a good indicator of public opinion, and it is essential to note in a church setting.

Shared Media

Shared media is the most prevalent and accessible in our social media–driven world. Shared media is the content you choose to share with the world online. Users can also share the content that you post. Churches have the opportunity to leverage the nature of digital platforms and media outlets such as Instagram, Facebook, Twitter, and Snapchat in the shared media space. Shared media is all about the digital space because it is an interactive environment; networks of people can easily exchange different information quickly and see the content you produce through a single click. You have the opportunity to encourage followers to share information for the church to their constituents through a shared media model. The concept of shared media is incredibly useful for a church because through users sharing your content, you can reach other local accounts, and information can spread fairly rapidly. Shared media is measurable by social media analytics built into those platforms: how much interaction was accounted for on a post, how many people viewed your profile, if you gained or lost followers from a post, how many people bookmarked or sent a post to someone else—the list goes on. The best part is that it is free! Users sharing posts is the virtual equivalent of word-of-mouth advertising: make a good impression to get a good impression.

Owned Media

Owned media is simply anything your church produces that does not fall into any of the three previous media buckets. Owned media includes content the church entirely created such as blogs, newsletters, websites, social media content, apps, stories, and emails. You do not pay for the placement of any of these examples because you own the platforms. Your church's owned landing pages and content are the media sources that are paid, earned, and shared to drive people. The benefits of owned media are that you have complete control over every aspect of it. A potential problem is that the only way people find owned media is if it is directly distributed or intentionally searched for by the individual. There is no accidental stumbling upon your website or media pages. Owned media needs help from the other three media types to increase awareness that it is even there. Owned media is measured by viewing your website's analytics and tracking traffic.

Owned media can typically be pretty informative, and this is where you can place details. Shared or paid media is relatively short on information, but it's fun and eye-catching. You should not make graphics with a ton of text and details—they should be eye-catching. Times New Roman twelve-point font over a picture discussing the church's mission or the reason for an event doesn't generate the wow factor you're after. Use these platforms as a chance to be creative in your graphic work, and place all details in the captions. Your paid and earned media are what drive people to your owned media. People on your media are there (or signed up for it) intentionally, so giving them all that information is appropriate on your web page or owned media.

Combination Considerations

Knowing how these four methods works is the first step in combining them and leveraging them for success in advertising your church. Think through how pairing various types will be beneficial for your church's needs. For example, pairing paid and shared media works well in the online landscape. Paying to boost your posts can reach more people and will likely result in having a better chance of being shared (the more people who see it, the more shares). If your church has a really strong online presence, this would be a good option for you. Thinking through these different combinations will usually give you the best outcome.

Before throwing out random parts of the PESO model, gather your team to create a content plan. Be strategic in determining what will work best for your church with the resources you have. For example, if social media is not that widely used at your church, leveraging shared media might not be the way to go. Making all the content related to a season of the church's advertising must be thought out and purposeful. Additionally, make sure that it lines up with your church's vision or mission statement and that it meets the ministry's intended goals.

You can be as creative and savvy as you want, but it is practically useless if it does not align with the mission. Before moving forward, ask yourself the following: What is the end goal? Who is your audience and what platforms do they use most? Besides your audience, whom do you want to pick up your content? What is your competition doing? Know your audience, know your mission, and know your platforms to best use the PESO model to your advantage.

Appendix C: Church Communication Survey Example

Surveying your church before you begin planning your marketing strategy is vital to your success. Surveying is an art form in and of itself. You will get useless data if you ask the wrong questions or have too many open-ended questions. Here is an example of a survey to consider.

1. What is your age?

   *Age slider

2. Gender (choose one)

   Male   Female   Prefer not to answer

3. How do you best receive news or content from [*name of the church*]?

☐ Facebook
☐ Instagram
☐ Email
☐ Text
☐ Website
☐ Bulletin
☐ Announcements during service
☐ Word of mouth
☐ Other

4. Rate the following statement: I receive information about events or serving opportunities in an appropriate, timely manner.

1: strongly disagree 5: Neither agree nor disagree 10: strongly agree

1   2   3   4   5   6   7   8   9   10

5. How satisfied are you with communication efforts at [name of the church]?

1: not satisfied 10: the most satisfied

1   2   3   4   5   6   7   8   9   10

6. What information are you interested in hearing about? Check all that apply.

☐ Service updates
☐ Kids' ministry
☐ Student ministry
☐ Missions
☐ Small groups
☐ Community opportunities
☐ Other

7. When you need to find information about something related to [name of the church], where do you get it?

☐ Website
☐ Instagram
☐ Facebook
☐ Bulletin
☐ Ask a friend
☐ Call the church
☐ Email
☐ Newsletter
☐ Other

8. Rate the following statement: [*Name of the church*] effectively communicates to the community about upcoming events.

    1: completely disagree 5: neutral 10: completely agree

    1   2   3   4   5   6   7   8   9   10

9. Rate [name of the church]'s communication effort: I understand the communication efforts of [*name of the church*].

    1: completely disagree 5: neutral 10: completely agree

    1   2   3   4   5   6   7   8   9   10

10. Does our social media convey who we are as a church?

    ☐ Yes
    ☐ No
    ☐ I do not use social media

11. Do you feel like you receive information and are included regarding decisions being made in the church?

    ☐ Yes
    ☐ No
    ☐ Comment:

12. Is there anything you would change about how we communicate to the congregation?

13. What priorities do you think the communication efforts should focus on?

14. Do you think the communication efforts of [*name of the church*] are inclusive to those who are visiting for the first time?

   ☐ Yes, communication efforts are intentionally inclusive of new visitors.
   ☐ No, communication efforts are primarily tailored to members.

15. How satisfied are you as a member of [*name of the church*]?

   ☐ Very satisfied
   ☐ Satisfied
   ☐ Neutral
   ☐ Not very satisfied
   ☐ Not satisfied at all

Appendix D: Exercises for Naming a Church

These exercises, helpful in naming a church or ministry, were inspired by *Don't Call It That: A Naming Workbook*, by Eli Altman, which I highly recommend purchasing a copy of and using when naming your church.

Step 1

Do not overthink it. Just put pen to paper and write down the idea behind your church in one sentence or phrase. If something doesn't stick, write down several things. The point is to just get started.

Step 2

Now, list at least fifteen silly names for your church. For example:

1. Action Verb Church
2. Wild Coyote Church
3. Church of the Vibe
4. Vibe Church

5. Lit Church
6. Fresh Church
7. Headstrong Church
8. Church of a Thousand Dances
9. Church in the Street
10. Street Church

It can be helpful to write down all the names that your church got wrong in the past. Irrelevant names, silly names, long names—put them all down.

Step 3

Then, explain why the names are incorrect. Are they too general? Are they too churchy?

Step 4

Make a list of all the names you like. Try to write down as many names as you can.

Step 5

Feel free to write about why you like the names. Then rank the names according to their likability.

Step 6

Imagine having this conversation at a church conference:

- "Hi, I am [*name*] from [*church name*]."
- "Hi, I am [*name*]. Tell me about your [*church name*]."
- "[*Church name*] is . . ."

And you take the story from there.

Does the church name make it easier to make introductions, or does it make it harder? Does it get people talking? Or does it keep them from asking you more questions?

Step 7

Take stock of the names by reflecting and doing some research on them:

1. Highlight your favorite names.
2. You may want to Google your church's name to determine whether there are any churches with the same or a very similar name in your city, and then Google the church's name within your state.
3. Check to see if the URL is available. You can buy domains at Google.com/domains. GoDaddy pricing might be cheap at first, but they tend to go up year after year. Google stays the same price consistently. Another great source for domain registration is PorkBun.com.
4. Make sure the URL you intend to use is not in violation of a trademark. You may want to consult an attorney who specializes in trademarks or use a trademark service online before proceeding with the name.
5. Protect your church's name as a valuable asset, like a building. Trademarks are name insurance, so you may want to go through the trademarking process.

Because church naming must lean on God's calling while also taking into account things like URL, SEO, and local competition for name longevity, it requires some creativity and science. It is not necessary to be Second Baptist Church or Mt. Carmel Baptist Church #2. That said, it is OK if that's what you ultimately decide is the best.

Appendix E: How to Create a Facebook Page and Group

How to Create a Facebook Page

1. Go to https://facebook.com/pages/create.
2. Type your church's name as the Page name.
3. Choose "Church" as the Page's category.
4. Type a page description of your church. You could use your church's mission statement.
5. Once you have entered the information, click "Create Page."
6. Now it is time to add your church logo and a Facebook cover image. The Page profile image dimensions are 500x500 pixels. A Facebook cover photo dimensions are 2050x780 pixels.
7. Once you add the pictures, Facebook will display a preview of your page.
8. When you are ready, click "Save," and you'll be taken to your new page.

Welcome to your church's new Facebook Page. You'll be able to further customize your Page using the left sidebar. Feel free to browse through those settings to see just how customizable your Page is.

How to Create a Facebook Group

To create a Group, first make sure the church already has a Facebook Page. Then create a Group that is linked to the church's Page so that every visitor to the church's Page can get easy access to all of the church's different Groups. It is an easy way to keep the church's Groups all in one place and connected.

These are the steps in creating a Facebook Group that is linked to the church's Facebook Page:

1. Go to the church's Facebook Page, and under the "More" tab, click "Groups."
2. After clicking "Groups," click "Create Linked Group."
3. Fill in the information about the church's Group. First, decide on and fill in the name of the Group (e.g., "First Baptist Members Group").
4. Choose either to make the church's Group public or private. Most recommendations are to set the Group to a private, visible Group. People will still be able to search and find the Group, but they will not see the content inside unless they join.
5. See that the Group is listed under "Groups" on the church's Page. To get to the Group, click the church's Group name under "Linked Groups."
6. Now the church has a Group. To change the Group's cover photo, click the "Edit" button. Then, upload a photo or image.
7. Now that the church has a basic Group set up, the church leader can fully customize the Group using the left sidebar. This sidebar is where one can approve members, set automatic approvals, set membership questions, approve or deny pending posts in the Group, create topics for posts, define group rules, and so much more.

A Facebook Group is a tool for building a community online. With Groups, it is straightforward to have an online community within a church. There are so many other things a church can do specifically with a Facebook Group. The church can also create Groups that serve shared interests outside the church as outreach. Facebook Groups can help the church reach its goals.

Appendix F: Nonprint and Traditional/Print Communication Methods

The church has been using print and media to communicate to their communities and congregations for hundreds of years. While many of these methods are considered older and more traditional, that does not mean they are less valid. On the contrary, there is something about the tangible nature of printed materials that offers a warm connection between people; it also offers an opportunity to create a piece of art. Traditional church communication methods generally consist of a weekly sermon, announcements, bulletin, print materials, and small groups.

Nonprint Communication Methods

The weekly sermon has been the primary means of communicating to congregations from the beginning. While it is not necessarily seen as a means of communicating in the sense that we use it in this book, it is probably the most critical and prevalent communication method in a church. Every church, pretty much everywhere, has a sermon every week—even online. Sermons can be used to sway and influence a congregation. They hold the most weight of any other communication piece and are often given the most time. When it comes to marketing, a marketer is looking for what type of content people pay attention to the longest. In the secular world, this would be a podcast. For a church, this would be a sermon. If the congregation spends the most time listening to the sermon, it must be clear and relevant. The more people listen to the sermon, the more they will understand and share their thoughts. Here are some best practices when constructing a sermon that communicates clearly:

- Use precise language and simple words.
- Create an outline that is easy to follow.
- Keep the points short but specific. Cut out unnecessary information.
- Make sure it is relevant.
- Make sure it is biblical.

A weekly sermon is not the only type of communication a church might have. Some announcements can be made to update congregants on what is going on in and around their community. Announcements involve more than just print material; they can include special events like concerts or lectures. Announcements can be tedious, but it is OK to get creative with them. For example, watch Jimmy Fallon's "Slow Jam the News" segment. It is relevant, memorable, and fun—the trinity of most viral content. Some best practices for church announcements include:

- Keep it short.
- Use a hook to make the announcements more exciting and relevant, like using the name of someone honored or involved with the event.
- Make it fun. Even a fresh face will add fun to Sunday morning.

A church might also have small groups, which are meeting times where members come together to talk about a Bible-based topic with other people in their group who share similar life circumstances or goals. These meetings can be used to strengthen one another by exchanging spiritual thoughts and encouraging words. It is also a way for church members to get more out of their Sunday morning service and learn how they can help people outside the congregation. Here are some best practices of using the church's small groups for communicating announcements and other necessary information to a church:

- Have a designated person keep in touch with the small group leaders and provide them with any necessary information to be shared. Be sure to keep the group leaders updated on any changes regarding who is leading a small group, how often they will be meeting, and the next steps for each of them.
- Create an announcement form that the church can distribute before each meeting to fill out what is being announced at the next meeting.
- Leave notes for those who have missed meetings so they know what happened at the meeting.

Traditional/Print Communication Methods

The bulletin is another traditional church communication method. It is usually a one- to two-page, black and white paper that includes the weekly sermon title with an introductory sentence or two to explain what the sermon will be about, announcements for the week including any activities happening at the church, and then the list of songs for worship. Bulletins have evolved quite a bit since the beginning of church history and the invention of the printing press. Today many bulletins include graphics and carry the church's branding. Here are some best practices for creating a church bulletin:

- Use colors and graphics to enhance the bulletin.
- Keep it clean; do not overdo images or words on a page.
- Do not to use more than two fonts.
- Be sure that any information is accurate before printing the bulletins.

Use the bulletin to keep people updated on what is going on in the congregation and community. The more the church tells them, the more they will know about it—and be interested in it too!

Printed media does not have the same reach as other methods, but it offers benefits difficult to replicate with other media—portability and longevity. The church can create books or pamphlets for congregants interested in learning more about their faith and spiritual practices.

These items are inexpensive to create and easy to distribute. Here are some instances when print should be used instead of a website:

- If the church is new and does not have a website
- When church members want more in-depth research about their spiritual practices
- For use as teaching tools or to supplement lessons at weekly Bible studies, Sunday school classes, or small group meetings

These traditional methods of communication for churches should not be ruled out. They are inexpensive and easy to create, and some best practices can help the church make them more effective. These best practices include:

- Be clear and concise.
- Use images, graphics, and charts to help illustrate the text where necessary.
- Limit to one font for all printed materials or use a typeface that is easy on the eyes (Garamond) when combining different fonts to create an appealing design.

What is old can be new again! Traditional church communication methods do not have to be overlooked but instead updated for today's culture. A lot has changed since the beginning of church history and the invention of the printing press:

- Bulletins now include graphics and carry a church's branding.
- There are more fonts to choose from on computers than in decades past.
- Printed media offers the advantage of portability and longevity.

It does not matter how old these methods are; they are still necessary for church communication today.

Appendix G: Budgeting

It is still disputed among churches why they should set aside part of their budgets and resources for communication. One recurring notion is that funding communication is not viewed as a ministry. However, the church is home to many missions, and communication makes those ministries possible. How communication is handled is a huge determinant of how the gospel is shared across all nations today.

No longer are flyers and pamphlets about upcoming services the only way to inform a church's members. No longer do members have to directly approach individuals to inform them about the gospel. Why not take advantage of the vast opportunities that communication offers today and translate it into recruiting new church members and engaging and serving existing church members?

Setting a Budget Is the First Step

Websites, advertisements, promotions, emails, or even text messages all require funding. The more a church is concerned with successfully delivering its message, the more resources are needed. It is understandable that for many churches this is a brand-new step. However, setting aside a budget that solely serves the purpose of supporting church communication can soon be very rewarding, with more engaged attendees as an outcome.

Setting up a website and automated text message reminders is one way to improve a church's communication strategy, but being truly engaged goes further than that. It takes a lot of effort to keep church members involved and even more to recruit new ones. Sending out emails, creating new content on the church website, managing a social media presence, and using text messages to contact people are all tasks that are part of communication. Considering the variety of available options and at what cost they come, having a budget available is significant for success.

One reasonable option is to have at least one person or a small team in a church that can take on this responsibility. Again, this can be a volunteer. It will be worth the investment, especially as you think of the long-term goal of keeping the gospel alive for future generations. In order to reach those future generations, churches must be up-to-date with their ways of communicating. Today and even more so in the future, people's schedules will be entirely run through their smartphones. Churches that know how to stay relevant and accessible today will most likely be successful in the future.

How to Set a Church Communication Budget

First, determine what the church's current communication needs are. Define the communication team's goals and objectives again. Most church budgets are set by "rule of thumb" or "basically what we did last year." Often churches will start with some arbitrary number and then increase or decrease depending on the previous years' spending. Is this the best method? Probably not. Is it the most common? Probably so. You can also take a more methodical approach and look at the list of events and ministries your church has and set aside equal budgets to promote and communicate those projects. This method is more meticulous but is often a better place to start than an arbitrary number. Have the church determine its ministries and events for the year, then the communication director can have a better chance at asking for the right budget to communicate about those things.

Second, estimate how much money is needed to meet those needs. Will the event need an ad budget? Will the communication team have to outsource some of the work? What does printing cost? Determine how much money will be spent on each area of communication (e.g., salaries, printing, mailing, email, social media). Then compare that estimate of a budget with what other departments are requesting, such as worship and outreach. Afterward, consider what would happen if a certain need went unmet due to lack of funds, and consider what expenses might need to be cut to make room for certain projects.

Bibliography

"About Public Relations." Public Relations Society of America. Accessed March 17, 2021. https://www.prsa.org/about/all-about-pr.

Allred, Katie, and Kenny Jahng. *Instagram Posts That Worked: Real-Life Examples from Church Communicators across the Country*. Self-published, Amazon.com, 2020.

"Brand." *Common Language Marketing Dictionary*. Accessed February 18, 2021. https://marketing-dictionary.org/b/brand.

Cairnes, Robert. "Measuring Your Church's Success on Social Media." Orange Leaders. March 23, 2017. https://orangeleaders.com/2017/03/23 /measuring-your-churchs-success-on-social-media.

Carmichael, Kayla. "Extending Marketing Mix: What It Is and Why It's Useful." *Hubspot Blog*, July 8, 2020. https://blog.hubspot.com/marketing /extended-marketing-mix.

Chandler, Diana. "Fastest-Growing, Largest Churches: Who Made the List?" Baptist Press. September 12, 2019. https://www.baptistpress.com/resource-library /news/fastest-growing-largest-churches-who-made-the-list.

"Church Communications Facebook Group." Facebook. Posted October 3, 2020. https://www.facebook.com/groups/churchcomm/ permalink/1499869570196636.

"Church and Religious Charitable Giving Statistics." Nonprofits Source. Accessed September 28, 2021. https://nonprofitssource.com/online-giving-statistics /church-giving.

Clark, Jerod. "Church Website Statistics." The Network. August 1, 2012. https:// network.crcna.org/church-web/church-website-statistics.

"Company Info." Facebook, February 10, 2021. https://about.fb.com/company-info.

Conrad, Andrew. "10 Powerful Church Statistics on Social Media Use." *Software Buying Tips and Advice for Businesses.* March 13, 2018. https://blog.capterra .com/church-statistics-social-media.

Constine, Josh. "A Year Later, $19 Billion for WhatsApp Doesn't Sound So Crazy." TechCrunch. February 20, 2015. https://techcrunch.com/2015/02/19 /crazy-like-a-facebook-fox.

Cox, Brandon. "33 Questions for Auditing Your Church's Social Media Effectiveness." Pastor Brandon Cox. February 4, 2015. https://brandonacox .com/dare-audit-churchs-communication-strategy-33-questions-ask.

Cox, Lindsay Kolowich. "16 Stats That Prove the Importance of Local SEO." *HubSpot Blog*, June 25, 2019. https://blog.hubspot.com/marketing /local-seo-stats.

Cullum, Steve. "6 Questions to Ask as You Are Naming Ministries/Programs." *Youth Specialties Blog*, March 30, 2020. https://blog.youthspecialties .com/6-questions-to-ask-as-you-are-naming-ministries-programs.

"Cyber Church: Pastors and the Internet." Barna Group. February 11, 2015. https:// www.barna.com/research/cyber-church-pastors-and-the-internet.

"Demographics of Social Media Users and Adoption in the United States." Pew Research Center: Internet, Science, and Tech. April 26, 2021. https://www .pewresearch.org/internet/fact-sheet/social-media.

"Definitions of Marketing." American Marketing Association. Accessed September 28, 2021. https://www.ama.org/the-definition-of-marketing-what-is-marketing.

Dietrich, Gini. "What Is the PESO Model? Integration of the Four Media Types." Spin Sucks. March 5, 2020. https://spinsucks.com/what-is-the-peso-model.

Elrod, Brandon. "Southern Baptists Organize to Help amid COVID-19 Crisis." Baptist Press. March 18, 2020. https://www.baptistpress.com/resource-library /news/southern-baptists-organize-to-help-amid-covid-19-crisis.

Felke-Morris, Terry. *Web Development and Design Foundations with HTML5.* London, UK: Pearson, January 2020.

"First Baptist Bryan." *Outreach Magazine.* June 26, 2019. https://outreachmagazine .com/church/first-baptist-bryan.

"Five Guys." Five Guys. Accessed September 2, 2021. http://www.fiveguys.com.

"Global Social Media Stats." DataReportal. Accessed September 28, 2021. https:// datareportal.com/social-media-users.

Godin, Seth. "What Is Marketing Today? With Seth Godin." YouTube, December 19, 2019. Video, 4:39. https://www.youtube.com/watch?v=vrJY85dBJLc.

Google Trends. "Prayer." Google Trends. August 19, 2020. https://trends.google .com/trends/explore?q=prayer&geo=US.

Gotter, Ana. "The 57+ Instagram Statistics You Need to Know in 2020." Ad Espresso. August 4, 2020. https://adespresso.com/blog/instagram-statistics.

Gould, Alexander. "Don't Overlook the Second Largest Search Engine Anymore." *Longview News Journal.* January 24, 2014. https://www.news-journal.com /news/local/dont-overlook-the-second-largest-search-engine-anymore/article _fb9fbc34-3874-597c-a68f-c527037619fd.html.

Grewal, Dhruv, and Michael Levy. *Marketing.* New York: McGraw Hill Education, 2020.

"A Guide to Disability Rights Laws." Americans with Disabilities Act. Accessed
    March 28, 2021. https://www.ada.gov/cguide.htm.

Haughey, Duncan. "A Brief History of SMART Goals." Project Smart. December
    13, 2014. https://www.projectsmart.co.uk/brief-history-of-smart-goals.php.

"History." Brentwood Baptist. Accessed March 17, 2021. https://brentwoodbaptist
    .com/about/history.

Hott, Allison. "40+ Email Marketing Statistics You Need to Know for 2021."
    OptinMonster. January 6, 2021. https://optinmonster.com
    /email-marketing-statistics.

"How Much Does Social Media Advertising Cost in 2021?" WebFX. Accessed
    September 28, 2021. https://www.webfx.com/how-much-does-social-media
    -advertising-cost.html.

Howse, Christopher. "A Furnace of Energy Whose Sermons Attracted Thousands."
    Telegraph. June 16, 2003. https://www.telegraph.co.uk/news/uknews/1433117
    /A-furnace-of-energy-whose-sermons-attracted-thousands.html.

"Instagram by the Numbers: Stats, Demographics, and Fun Facts." Omnicore.
    Accessed March 22, 2021. https://www.omnicoreagency.com
    /instagram-statistics.

International Organization for Standardization. "Brand Evaluation—Principles and
    Fundamentals." ISO. Accessed September 28, 2019. https://www.iso.org/obp
    /ui/#iso:std:iso:20671:ed-1:v1:en.

"Introduction to Web Accessibility." Web Accessibility Initiative (WAI). Accessed
    March 28, 2021. https://www.w3.org/WAI/fundamentals/accessibility-intro.

"Is Social Media Worth It? Measuring Social Media ROI for Churches." Social
    Church. May 8, 2019. https://socialchurch.com
    /is-social-media-worth-it-measuring-social-media-roi-for-churches.

Johnson, Caitlin. "Cutting through Advertising Clutter." CBS News. September 17,
    2006. https://www.cbsnews.com/news/cutting-through-advertising-clutter.

Kirkpatrick, David. "Study: Personalized Email Subject Lines Increase Open
    Rates by 50%." Marketing Dive. September 12, 2017. https://www
    .marketingdive.com/news/study-personalized-email-subject-lines-increase
    -open-rates-by-50/504714.

Kovach, Steve. "TikTok Deal Puts U.S. Owners in Charge, but Chinese Parent
    Company Still Has Some Say." CNBC. September 21, 2020. https://www.cnbc
    .com/2020/09/21/tiktok-deal-splits-control-between-us-and-chinese-owners
    .html.

Laja, Peep. "First Impressions Matter: Why Great Visual Design Is Essential." CXL.
    September 25, 2020. https://cxl.com/blog
    /first-impressions-matter-the-importance-of-great-visual-design.

"Loneliness and the Impact." Cigna. January 2019. https://www.cigna.com/static
    /www-cigna-com/docs/health-care-providers/resources/loneliness-index
    -provider-flyer.pdf.

Lucid Content Team. "Agile vs. Waterfall vs. Kanban vs. Scrum." *Lucidchart Blog*,
    October 9, 2019. https://www.lucidchart.com/blog
    /agile-vs-waterfall-vs-kanban-vs-scrum.

Mawhinney, Jesse. "50 Visual Content Marketing Statistics You Should Know in 2021." *HubSpot Blog*, February 16, 2021. https://blog.hubspot.com/marketing /visual-content-marketing-strategy.

"MII University." Media Impact International. Accessed September 2, 2021. https:// www.mii.global.

Miller, Donald. *Building a StoryBrand: Clarify Your Message so Customers Will Listen.* New York: HarperCollins Leadership, 2017.

Minnick, Jessica. *Responsive Web Design with HTML 5 & CSS.* 9th ed. Boston, MA: Cengage Learning, 2020.

Ninivaggi, Frank J. "Loneliness: A New Epidemic in the USA." *Psychology Today.* February 12, 2019. https://www.psychologytoday.com/us/blog/envy/201902 /loneliness-new-epidemic-in-the-usa.

O'Dea, Simon. "Forecast Number of Mobile Users Worldwide 2020–2024." Statista. September 22, 2020. https://www.statista.com/statistics/218984 /number-of-global-mobile-users-since-2010.

"Our Story." Central Baptist. Accessed March 19, 2021. https://centralbaptist.com /ourstory.

"Our Story: First Baptist Jackson." First Baptist Jackson. Accessed March 19, 2021. https://www.firstbaptistjackson.org/our-story.

Perrin, Andrew, and Madhu Kumar. "About Three-in-Ten U.S. Adults Say They Are 'Almost Constantly' Online." Pew Research Center. May 30, 2020. https:// www.pewresearch.org/fact-tank/2019/07/25 /americans-going-online-almost-constantly.

Ross, Wilbur. "Commerce Department Prohibits WeChat and TikTok Transactions to Protect the National Security of the United States." Street Insider. September 18, 2020. https://www.streetinsider.com/Mergers+and+Acquisitions /Commerce+Department+Prohibits+WeChat+and+TikTok+Transactions+to +Protect+the+National+Security+of+the+United+States/17372727.html.

"Sample Church Press Release Outline." Peninsula-Delaware Conference of the United Methodist Church. Accessed March 28, 2021. https://www.pen-del.org /files/content/sample+pendel+church+press+release+outline.docx.

Santora, Jacinda. "Is Email Marketing Dead? Statistics Say: Not a Chance." OptinMonster. August 14, 2020. https://optinmonster.com /is-email-marketing-dead-heres-what-the-statistics-show.

"Second Baptist Church." Outreach 100. Accessed March 19, 2021. https:// outreach100.com/churches/second-baptist-church-1.

Shearer, Brady. "Social Media Policy for Churches: The Definitive Guide." *Nucleus Blog*, September 1, 2020. https://www.nucleus.church/blog /social-media-policy-churches.

Sinek, Simon. *Start with Why: How Great Leaders Inspire Everyone to Take Action.* London: Penguin Business, 2019.

Smietana, Bob. "Most Churches Offer WiFi but Skip Twitter." Lifeway Research. January 9, 2018. https://lifewayresearch.com/2018/01/09 /most-churches-offer-free-wi-fi-but-skip-twitter.

Smith, Aaron, and Monica Anderson. "Social Media Use in 2018." Pew Research Center. March 1, 2018. https://www.pewresearch.org/internet/wp-content /uploads/sites/9/2018/02/PI_2018.03.01_Social-Media_FINAL.pdf.

Statista Research Department. "U.S. Snapchat Usage by Age 2020." Statista. January 28, 2021. https://www.statista.com/statistics/814300 /snapchat-users-in-the-united-states-by-age.

Sweaza, Dan. "Church Communications Facebook Group." Facebook. Accessed March 15, 2021. https://www.facebook.com/groups/churchcomm /permalink/1499869570196636.

Tankovska, H. "U.S. Snapchat Usage by Age 2020." Statista. January 28, 2021. https://www.statista.com/statistics/814300 /snapchat-users-in-the-united-states-by-age.

"The 5 Ws (and 1 H) That Should Be Asked of Every Project!" Workfront. May 7, 2018. https://www.workfront.com/blog/project-management-101-the-5-ws-and -1-h-that-should-be-asked-of-every-project.

Turner, Erica, and Lee Rainie. "Most Americans Rely on Their Own Research to Make Big Decisions, and That Often Means Online Searches." Pew Research Center. March 5, 2020. https://www.pewresearch.org/fact-tank/2020/03/05 /most-americans-rely-on-their-own-research-to-make-big-decisions-and-that -often-means-online-searches.

"Vision." Bellevue. Accessed August 25, 2021. https://www.bellevue.org/vision.

"Vision and Values." Redemption Church. Accessed March 22, 2021. https://www .redemptiontx.com/vision.

"Web Content Accessibility Guidelines (WCAG) Overview." Web Accessibility Initiative (WAI). Accessed March 28, 2021. https://www.w3.org/WAI /standards-guidelines/wcag.

Weinschenk, Susan. *100 Things Every Designer Needs to Know about People.* San Francisco: New Riders, 2020.

"What Is an SSL Certificate?" GlobalSign GMO Internet. October 22, 2020. https:// www.globalsign.com/en/ssl-information-center/what-is-an-ssl-certificate.

"YouTube." YouTube. Accessed March 22, 2021. https://www.youtube.com/intl /en-GB/about.

"YouTube: The 2nd Largest Search Engine (Infographic)." Mushroom Networks. Accessed March 22, 2021. https://www.mushroomnetworks.com/infographics /youtube---the-2nd-largest-search-engine-infographic.

Name and Subject Index